# MOJO from the KARATE DOJO

## INSIGHTFUL LIFE LESSONS

### BY
### KARATE SENSEI
### DWAYNE WEIDENDORF

When I first started putting pen to paper my main objective was to write a memoir for my children. It was an excellent opportunity for me to share some good life lessons that I have learned from my karate training over the past 30 years. When I started accumulating some thickness from the pages that I had written, I went to Lance Perverley, Beau Simpson and Frank Bucholtz — all award-winning editors who gave me the encouragement to put this memoir in a book format. They all believed that this would be a very unique read that had the ability to connect with a broad non-martial arts audience. Thanks to all three of you for the guidance and the positive feedback that allowed me to push this project forward. Thanks also to Marla Poirier who is amazingly creative and is the artist who designed the cover and contents of "Mojo from the Karate Dojo". I would also like to give acknowledgement to reporter and book author Tom Zytaruk for helping me with the title. Thank you to reporter Nick Greenizan for allowing me to use a quote or two from one his of his sport stories and a big thank you to Frank and Bonnie Bucholtz who officially edited my material. My gratitude also goes to Sensei Don Owens and Sensei Bill Bazeley two world class teachers who have shown me "the way". Also, I would like to thank all the students I have taught and a big salute to all the fellow martial artist that I have been so lucky to train with. Your guidance and friendships has made me who I am today.

My main objective is to give the reader some good advice that I have learned through my karate experiences. Lessons that can help and support you on your very own life journey. If you really wanted to, I bet you could read this book in a couple of nights. However, I would highly suggest that you take your time with it and read a couple of chapters at a time and digest the material and see if you can incorporate the lessons in your very own life. After the read, if you have learned just one new lesson that you can apply in your life from the material I have written , I will consider my project a success. Thanks for taking the time out of your busy schedule to read my book. I hope you get a "kick" out of "Mojo from the Karate Dojo".

This book is dedicated to my wife Lorraine and my children Drew and Bree.

Sensei Dwayne Weidendorf is a fourth-degree black belt in karate and has over 30 years of multi-disciplinary training. He is an advance instructor in both Shotokan and Wado-Ryu Karate and has an excellent background in self-defence, which gives him great insight into the martial arts. Sensei Dwayne has the ability to connect with students of all levels and has had an instrumental influence on everyone he teaches. His positive attitude has always been contagious and his unique ability to put words on paper is inspiring. The life lessons that he has shared in his book is not only for the martial artist, but is purposely geared towards everyone who ever wanted some good wholesome guidance.

## Hanshi Don Owens大将軍
9th degree Black Belt and Vice President of the World Japan Karate Association

President of the International Shotokan Ryu Karate Do Shihankai

Order of the Scottish Samurai (Great Shogun)

ISBN: 978-1-9992865-0-7
First published November 2019

# — Table of Contents —

# Forward

Life can be an amazing journey full of joy and happiness. Along the way you will come up against many roadblocks and it's up to you to leap frog over these challenges to continue on your path to success. With the right tools successful people learn to turn their challenges into positive learning experiences and build the foundation for their lives around this knowledge. It's these experiences (if used properly) that enable individuals to grow and get the most out of life.

Many successful individuals have outlets that they have built their own personal foundations around. It could be a sport, music, arts or in some cases a really good mentor. They use these channels to successfully learn how to conduct themselves through good and bad times on their road to success. For me personally, karate became the outlet that allowed me to grow into the person I am today. It's the rock that I turn to when I need to use it the most. I use karate everyday — maybe not in a physical sense, but in a mind, body and spirit connectivity that enables me to be the best that I can be.

This book happened by chance. About seven years ago, I began to feed my love for writing and started to scribble some "Life Lessons" that I have learned from my Karate training. I wanted to share some of these lessons with my children and really let them know who their Dad really was. I have an amazing family and I love being a Dad, but I lived a busy life being a business owner, media executive, marital artists, and at times, I felt I left that void of giving them the proper mentorship that I always craved for. After having over 30 pieces written, I went to some of my friends who were award winning editors and told them what I was up to with my scribbles. They both looked at me and told me that I have a story to tell and that I should share it with the general public in a book format.

After many days and nights of hitting the keyboard, I'm elated to have a book that I can share with you some of the life lessons I have learned from my thirty plus years of karate training. My target audience from the conception of this idea was not the martial artist, but the general public as a whole. These karate lessons that I have learned can be used by everyone in all walks of life to help people get through their own personal journey. These lessons are what I have built my own personal foundation on and I trust that you too can enjoy the benefits of these readings.

I would like to thank my wife Lorraine, son Drew and daughter

Bree for being there with me every step of the way. To my editor (and friend) Frank Bucholtz for believing in me and giving me the guidance to pursue this project. To my karate mentors, Sensei Bazeley and Sensei Owens for giving me the instruction and knowledge to grow as karate student and most importantly as a person. I will be forever grateful to them. I dedicate this project to everyone who is taking the time to read this book while having an open mind to learn some of the life lessons I have experienced in the pages of "Mojo in The Karate Dojo".

# Introduction

## Life Lessons in Karate

When the movie "The Karate Kid" came out in theatres in 1984, I was instantly inspired. I wanted to be the next "Karate Kid." I was athletic growing up, but a bit undersized and really didn't grow until my late teen years. My first objective when I signed up for some Kung-Fu lessons in the mid-1980's was to master some cool moves so I could learn to fight and defend myself. Little did I know martial arts would become an integral part of my life. It has been a lifelong commitment which has had tremendous influence on my development as a professional and as a human being.

I proudly hold a fourth-degree black belt in Shotokan Karate through the World Japan Karate Association and a fourth-degree black belt in Wado-Ryu Karate. I have been training for over 30 years and have had the pleasure of owning my own karate dojo. I have also trained several hundred students throughout my martial arts career and have been very fortunate and grateful to be mentored and taught by two of the very best traditional karate instructors in the world. I owe the world to my Wado Sensei Bill Bazeley and my Shotokan Hanshi Don Owens – without them my journey would never had a start or finish line. Karate is more than a fighting art. It is a way of life which can contribute to the betterment of your mind, body and spirit.

The most popular question junior students ask me is, "Have you ever used your karate?" My reply is short and sweet, "I use it every day." Karate has given me valuable lessons throughout the years which have led directly to the successes I have had in my professional and private life. Karate has been the core foundation around which I have built my entire life philosophy, and I can honestly say that karate has transformed my life. It's the edge that I believe many experienced martial artists have over their peer groups. Throughout my professional career as an executive, I have had the opportunity to work with several different successful business owners, high performing executives and athletes. I have found there was a direct correlation between successful people and the core life lessons I have learned through karate.

In the following chapters, I will share with you some of these "life lessons" that I learned through karate. I believe these lessons will give you the edge you need in your life-long journey. No need for the blood, sweat and tears needed to participate in the dojo, all you need is an open mind and a willingness to learn to master some the best life lessons that I have grasped.

Now kick back in your chair, block out all negativity and I trust that you will enjoy the punch that my personal karate experience has taught me in the past 30 years of training.

## 2

# Karate-do

**"It's how we overcome those challenges that make us better and helps us navigate through life."**

The word karate is a combination of two Chinese characters: Kara, meaning empty and te means hand; thus, the definition translates to "empty hand." The do translates to the "The way or path." The term karate ("empty hand") means fighting in combat with your hands and feet without the use of weapons. Do ("The Way or Path") brings karate to life and explains that karate is much more than a fighting art. It's a lifestyle that can guide and teach us through our life-long journey.

Life in fact is a journey, and each and every one of us finds "a way or path." For some the path is clear and takes you through many obstacles that you are able to overcome and conquer, leading to success and happiness. For others, the path can be challenging and often individuals lose focus and get off the path. This can often be very destructive and lead to stresses, mental health issues and substance abuse. I like to refer to it as the "off the rails" syndrome. In the very worst cases, those people who are completely off the rails are so far off that they will need help to get them back on track. If they don't make the decision to help themselves and reach out to others to get professional help, they become lost. They are never able to reach their full potential and are destined to failure. Their situation often becomes dire and can lead to a crash.

We are all human and struggle at different intervals during our life-long journey. Perhaps you have been diagnosed with a serious health problem, lost your job, have challenges with your relationship, lost a loved one, or are in financial hardship. Challenges happen to all of us, but it's how do we deal with this adversity that counts. Most of us are able to reach out and get some help to support us. Others lean on our families, friends, professionals or even religion for some much-needed support. Karate-do has been much more than a fighting art to me. It's been "a way or path" that navigates me through good and bad times. I have been through many life challenges, but karate has always been there for me giving me the direction I need to get back on the rails. When you are reading through this book, have an open mind and look at your life through the lens of a senior karate teacher. Think of your life as a journey. Be honest with yourself, question yourself and evaluate your very own "way or path." Are you happy with your current life or would you like to change course? The good news is you hold the power as your very own personal decision maker and can change your path by making positive decisions that will guide you through life. Never be discouraged, because we all will come up against challenges. It's how we overcome those challenges that enhances our personal development and encourages us to navigate through our life.

Using the analogy of a stream, your life might get rocky at times. You will have moments of hot and cold just like the water. You will also experience many ebbs, flows, turns, and obstacles that you will need to navigate before you reach your final destiny. Just like the stream, you will continue to flow down your very own personal passage, creating your very own way. By making good decisions and finding your passions you will benefit by getting the most out of your life. Karate-do is has ben an exhilarating path for my own personal development. Just like me, you will come against roadblocks that you need to overcome in your life. This makes the course even more satisfying. My goal is to share with you some of the personal karate lessons I have learned through my training. They can help and support you on your very own way through life.

# 3

# The Power of a Positive Mind

**"You can do anything if you put your mind to it."**

We all know that one person (or maybe two) who exhibits a continuous negative attitude. They are complainers, whiners, find fault and often raise a stink with just about everything. I refer to this sad type of behavior as "poison" and we all know what kind of toxic environment this type of person can create for themselves and others. On the contrary, we all know that one person who exhibits a positive aura about them as they always strive to find the positive in everything they do in life. We often feed off their positive energy and envy the way they go about their way in life. It's without question that negative thoughts will always result in damaging outcomes and positive thoughts will equate to positive results.

Karate has taught me that anything in life is possible if you stay positive and focused. Karate at times can be very overwhelming and intimidating, especially when you first start training. Many of your superiors are performing techniques that the everyday average person could not even fathom performing. I remember working with a group of senior karate students breaking down the all-impressive "spin hook kick." I was instantly amazed at how quick and efficient these experts were performing this kick. Then I accidently blurted out "There is no way I will be able to perform that kick." My head sensei came over and immediately scolded me and said "Don't ever tell me you can't do something – If you put your mind to it you can do anything." I naturally felt a bit humiliated at the moment, but I actually listened to the message, swallowed my pride and started to focus on a positive "I can" attitude. In the end, after many weeks of training, the "spin hook kick" became not only my favorite technique but also my go-to fighting kick.

I have a dear friend who is a high-ranking black belt. He went through some very difficult times fighting brain cancer. He could have given up but he decided to take a positive attitude towards this challenging time in his life. He was able to use the power of his positive thinking to conquer his cancer. He has been cancer-free for many years and continues to train harder than anyone I know. As a senior karate teacher, he always exhibits a positive attitude inside and outside of the class. We all get an inspiring lift from him when we see him, because he lives his life to the fullest and lights up a room with the positive energy that he continually displays. Life is full of challenges and we all face adversity in life, but always remember to go above and beyond the call of duty for yourself. Strive to be positive and find solutions that will get you back on track.

The point is this: Anyone can achieve anything they desire with a positive attitude. You are ultimately in control of your very own destiny. By making good choices and staying focused you can accomplish anything if you put your mind to it. Individuals often put barriers up and get in their own way by not creating positive thoughts. You are in control of your own future, so you need to get a grip on your life and embrace the power of positive thinking. Next time you have negative thoughts, it's okay to feel and understand those negative thoughts. Ultimately, push through them and try and find solutions that will overcome and destroy the negativity. Visualize and believe in positive outcomes. You only have one life to live so make sure you don't waste time beating yourself or others up. Just like my karate colleague who fought the hard battle of overcoming brain cancer, you too can use positive thinking as a lifelong tool that will provide you with fulfillment, joy and happiness.

4

# Conquer Your Fears

**"By facing your fears you will be able to overcome any obstacle that life throws at you."**

Fear often holds people back and can get in the way of their success. It can paralyze you or it can act as a motivation to move you forward to overcome your specific worry. There are several different types of fears. These include fear of failure, fear of change, fear of losing, fear of being judged, fear of bad things happening to you, fear of heights, fear of insects - and the list goes on. Everyone experiences fear, but we all manage it differently. By taking action, you can learn to understand your angst and come up with an action plan to overpower it and move forward in a positive way.

My karate experience has showed me the importance of accepting my personal fears, and facing the adversity that comes with them. When I first started training, I had the fear of being judged and I also feared getting hurt. It took me several months before I broke through these barriers and accepted myself for who I was, while confronting my fears head on. I learned that the best way to overcome my fear of getting physically hurt was to engage in some light sparring and feel the pain of a punch or two. It was intimidating at first, but this fighting experience gave me the building block to allow my confidence to increase and be completely comfortable with taking blows. I was also afraid of people judging me for my imperfections, but I soon learned that one of the core principles of martial arts is not to judge individuals. After several months of training, I became very at ease in my classes and I broke through this apprehensiveness. I became very comfortable in my skin and I was never again afraid of what others thought about me.

This is a very powerful lesson that I learned through karate - it's okay to experience fear, but it's also equally okay to face your fears and conquer them.

I see many people in today's society getting in their own way, by allowing fear to take over their entire life. It can create huge barriers for individuals and in the very worst case it can destroy the human spirit. I had the pleasure of working with a very talented sales representative at my office. She had amazing communication skills and plenty of energy and enthusiasm to go along with her bubbly personality. The only challenge was, she had a fear of going to see new clients. This was holding her back financially and professionally. By overcoming the fear of walking into to meet new clients, she was able to sell more and grow her business. She is now totally comfortable with walking in to meet new clients and by taking action she was able to change her behavior and turn it into a positive. My karate training has taught me that it's okay to feel the fear, but it's critical that you take action and face fear head on.

I have some very helpful tips for you to help yourself overcome your fears.

1. It's very normal to have fears. Learn to accept them. Everyone has anxieties - the question is how do you overcome yours and turn it into a positive?

2. Analyze your fears. Why are you experiencing these fears? Has a past experience been holding you back?

3. Derive a plan to conquer your fears head on. Ask yourself, what is the worst thing that can happen to me if I face my fear? Often you will find the reward outweighs the risk.

4. Take small steps to start your conquering process. If you are afraid of heights, you may want to start to climb a small hill before you conquer the mountain. Remember - one step at a time.

5. You are the only one that can change you or the way you look at things. If you wait for someone else to change the way you think, you will be waiting a lifetime.

6. Once you have taken steps to conquer your anxieties, reward yourself and feel the exhilaration and satisfaction that will follow.

7. If you are stuck and just can't do it yourself, seek the support of family, friends or professional help.

Standing in the ring with a superior karate fighter can be a very intimidating and humbling experience. Karate-do has taught me that it's okay to experience fear, but it's also important to stay strong and learn to fight your opponent face to face. By learning to face your fears, you will be able to overcome any obstacle that life throws at you. Life has no barriers or limits. By conquering your fears, you will turn paralyzing thoughts into positive and motivating outcomes.

# 5

# Back to Basics

**"A good karate stance must be solid because it gives you the foundation to perform good sound techniques."**

The quest to become a black belt in karate can be a very long, arduous process that takes perseverance, strategic goal setting and a significant time commitment. When I tested for my first degree (shodan) black belt, I was grilled through a three-hour exam which tested all the skills I had acquired over seven years of training. During the belt presentation, sensei Bazeley congratulated my colleagues and I on our passing and humbly informed us that we all now officially knew all the core karate basics.

He told us "Your first-degree black belt symbolizes the basic foundations that you need to continue your development in karate and learn more advanced techniques." I was dumbfounded, as I thought I was the real deal and a complete karate expert after my promotion. In fact, I had just learned the basics and was at the beginning stages of this life-long journey.

Years later, when I was a third-degree (sandan) black belt, I attended a karate seminar in Vancouver conducted by an eighth-degree karate expert from Japan. When I entered the dojo, I was quite excited about learning some new advanced techniques from this master. I was shocked when he commented that we would be working on basic beginner techniques like blocking, kicking, punching and stances for the entire class. Why would senior black belts go to an advanced seminar to work on basic techniques? I soon learned that the basics I had learned several years ago needed to be corrected and improved. I was instantaneously rewarded for having an open mind and working on the basic delivery of my moves. My skill improved, I was becoming more masterful in my movements and most importantly, I just learned a life-long lesson that will help guide me through my life.

It's like the analogy of the karate stance. A good karate stance must be solid because it gives you the foundation to perform good sound techniques. A good example of this is a well-built house that needs a solid foundation, so it will stand the outside environmental elements and won't fall to the ground when stressed. Sloppy karate stances will produce lackadaisical techniques. I took this philosophy of "Back to Basics" and applied it to my everyday life. When I get in a rut and need a boost, I take a step back, evaluate, and go back to the basics that I have learned in any of my chosen activities. It's like hitting the rewind button, giving you instant stimulus needed to improve your personal development.

I'm very blessed to live in British Columbia, Canada, which is one of the most mountainous, geographically scenic, and beautiful environments in the world. I have been skiing since I learned to walk and enjoy the sport immensely. I was on a ski trip a couple of years back with a friend who was an intermediate skier, and we spent a few days at Whistler skiing the long beginner and intermediate runs. The conditions were powdery and spectacular, and my friend and I were working consistently on our basic turns, balance, weigh-shifting, tempo and alignment — all basic techniques that allow the advanced skier to conquer any mountain. My friend was doing an absolute fantastic job on the beginner and intermediate runs, mostly due to him working on his basics. As soon as we went to an advanced run, he panicked and started to become shaky (landing a few spectacular wipe-outs) and his tempo and form became very sloppy. What was the problem? The issue was he lost his confidence and stopped working on the basics we had been working on in the past couple of days. Once we spent some time drilling down on his problems, and by simply applying his basic ski techniques, he started to improve immediately and was able to conquer the big mountain experience. His basic ski training allowed him to comfortably move to the next level of difficulty. As an advanced skier and a karate teacher, I constantly refine and work on my basic skills to become sharper and improve my skill.

You can apply this lesson in your everyday life, if you allow it. It will become an essential building block of the foundation you are building for yourself. For example, if you are a writer and are grappling with your craft you may want to evaluate some of the basics you have learned about grammar, structure, writing and reading techniques to get you back on track. If you are a musician and are struggling with your pieces, you may want to go back and review your basic note patterns, chords or playing techniques. If you are a hockey player and are in a rut with your game, go back to your basic hockey techniques like skating, shooting or passing to find your way. Don't be afraid to drill down and evaluate your performance at the most finite level. Perhaps you need to adjust your hip movement a few percentage points or your timing is off by a few milliseconds. By having an open mind, you can lean on your fundamental basic training skills and make improvements in your chosen activity immediately.

The great thing is you can take this "back to basics" approach to almost everything you do in life, including work, school, sport or music. Next time you hit the wall and need inspiration, take a step back, evaluate the issue, and go "back to basics" to get you on track. Basics techniques in karate are important to even the most senior sensei (teacher) and they must be practised and repeated on a regular basis to continue on your path to success. It's a karate lesson that will always be there for you, and it will give you the power to change your life for the better.

# 6

# Confident and Not Cocky

**"The recipe for success is to sprinkle just enough confidence to come across as self-assured in your respective abilities."**

Having confidence is an essential trait that every successful person needs in their arsenal, in order to perform at the highest possible level. The ability to feel good about yourself and be self-assured that you can conquer any obstacle standing in your way is very important. Confidence is defined as someone having self-assurance and appreciation of one's own ability. In karate, you learn to become confident in your abilities as a martial artist, but always remember, there is a fine line between having enough confidence and having too much.

There is no question that a person with 100 per cent confidence in their abilities will be successful in life. On the contrary, someone without that self-belief will find doubts and create barriers that won't allow them to truly realize their full potential. Although confidence is essential for success, there is a very fine line between confidence and cocky. Someone who is cocky thinks too highly of themselves and can often be described as being conceited, arrogant or overbearing. We all know a person who comes across this way, and who is ultimately handicapping themselves with this disrespectful aura. The key is finding a balance, so a person believes in themselves and their abilities without coming across as arrogant or possibly overbearing, creating social barriers.

When I first started taking karate, I quickly learned to check my overly-inflated ego at the door. I discovered the old-fashioned karate way (the Old butt kicking method) and soon learned that I wasn't as tough as I had believed I was. I vividly remember being schooled one evening while sparring with a young female black belt who was, in my mind, inferior to me in size, strength and fighting ability. Within 30 seconds of our match, I was hit with a spin side-kick to the ribs and had the wind totally knocked out of me. It was one of the most frightening moments of my life, as I unable to breathe properly for at least a minute. I walked out of the dojo that night with my tail between my legs and a deflated ego. I had learned a life-changing lesson. I wasn't as good as I thought I was, and this defeat gave me a whole new perspective on the difference between confidence and cocky. On the other hand, this young talented female martial artist who brought me to my knees had just the right amount of confidence in her abilities to defeat a male twice her size and strength. She never once exemplified an ounce of cockiness before or after our match.

It's extremely important for an individual to demonstrate confidence in everything they do in life. The recipe for success is to sprinkle just enough confidence to come across as self-assured in your respective abilities. With it, you can accomplish anything life throws at you. Sprinkle too much confidence in your repertoire and you will be perceived as cocky, which will put social barriers up for you that will get in your way. Without confidence, you will never truly realize your full potential. Striking this balance between confidence and cocky is a fine line, but once you are there it will allow you to move mountains and will provide you with a platform that will allow you to be the best that you can be. The experienced karate student has that sureness about their ability to allow them to execute karate at a high level, without coming across as arrogant. You too can use confidence as a building block to launch yourself to success. Just remember to keep it in check, when it becomes overbearing.

## 7

# Kime

**"With it you can conquer and achieve anything you desire"**

Kime is a Japanese term that means power. In karate, it's a highly-used term that means "focus." It's a concept that karate instructors practise on a regular basis to achieve the ultimate technique in fighting (kumite) and in patterns (kata).

Kata is defined as a series of karate techniques performed by martial artists that enable the student to continually practise and hone their technique through repetition. It's like a series of dance moves that takes years and years to master. It's a key component to the continual development process of a karate practitioner, as they are continually striving to improve by getting constantly critiqued by their teacher. The "kime" refers to the focus, quickness, power, energy, sharpness and timing of the movements. Without good "kime," the kata will be flat, un-exciting and lifeless. With it, the kata becomes alive and full of energy and enthusiasm. It's like watching a professional dancer mastering and displaying their art.

When sparring (fighting), the karate master will be alive and well, using energy, confidence and enthusiasm to overtake their opponent. They will appear to be in total control of their match and their techniques will be clean powerful, and fluid. Watching a karate expert utilize "kime" in either kata or kumite is like watching someone perform at the highest level of their mastery. They are the "crème de la crème" of karate supremacy. Without it they look clumsy, awkward, intimidated, and ultimately, ineffective.

What lessons can the average person learn from kime? Personally, I feel the most important aspect is the focus and energy component. I see too many individuals in everyday life not putting in 100 per cent effort- they take short-cuts and are unmotivated. For an example, take a below-average sales representative who goes to a sales call not totally prepared. My wife and I (as qualified buyers) went shopping for a vehicle recently and were very underwhelmed by the car sales person. He was very unengaging and not completely focused on the job at hand, as he handed us a key to the car without taking the time to ask us questions. As we sat in the car with no sales representative in sight, we quickly decided that this dealership was not the one we wanted to deal with. The call totally lacked focus, passion and we could tell this particular sales person was uninterested in us and lacked good old "kime".

We then crossed the road to a competing dealership and were overwhelmed with a caring sales representative. He had great product knowledge, was passionate about his product and genuinely cared about our wants and needs, displaying excellent "kime." Not surprisingly, we bought a vehicle from him on the spot and have been satisfied ever since.

You can also see this at your local sports field. As a soccer Dad, I constantly see children at the pitch not being focused and lacking energy for the task at hand. I also see children (even at a very young age) displaying excellent "kime" by being focused and displaying good energy and enthusiasm. In most cases, these are the athletes who excel and naturally become high-performers. They want it and will put 100% into their respective training to reach their goals

Performing at the highest level in any activity takes immense focus, energy and time to master. The old adage, "If you put your mind to it you can do anything" is true, especially if you bring the energy and focus needed to perform your aspiration. Without it, the only person you are cheating is yourself. You will continue to perform at a bare minimal level and will not attain the success you deserve. With it you can conquer and achieve anything you desire. So now is a good time to set a goal, make a plan and put all the focus and energy needed to master your skill. Be prepared to go "all in" and remember like a karate kata, "kime" can take years to master. High performers all utilize "kime" in their respective activities by being focused and exuding positive energy, confidence and enthusiasm, so they can perform at the elite level. Take the steps needed to incorporate "kime" in your life and just like the karate master, it will give you the edge to become the best that you can become in your chosen activity – 100 per cent guaranteed.

## 8

# Conflict Resolution — "Be The Willow Tree"

**"The Willow Tree is soft and will bend while the Oak tree is hard and will not budge."**

Every human at some time in their lives experiences disagreements, varying opinions, controversy, disputes and even heated arguments with other individuals. What makes life great is we are all unique. We have different character make-up, opinions and personalities. All of this hopefully contributes to a more positive and productive world. As a media executive, I have always accepted the fact that I am a public target and I learned through my karate training that everyone is entitled to their respective opinion, whether I agree or disagree. If a reader, advertiser, employee or member of the community wants to express their opinion to me, then I need to listen and respect them. It's those uncomfortable heated disagreements that are often harder to manage. Have you ever had a heated argument? Has anyone unfairly yelled at you or disrespected you? How have you managed this situation? How did you feel after the disagreement? Was it worth the effort? In most cases, people don't feel real great after an argument and there is often no amicable resolve, so the problem continues to fester. No one wins an argument.

Doju Kun in Japanese literally means "the club rules." In our karate club, two of our club rules are: refrain from violent behaviour and respect others. These club rules could make a big difference in how you approach conflict in the future.

I have had the pleasure of training with many experienced karate professionals who have never broken an ounce of sweat or drawn a drop of blood during a street fight. In fact, many of them have never been in a street fight and have mastered the "Willow Tree" philosophy. When a conflicting situation arises, they have the training to utilize their conflict resolution skills to avoid a disagreement and to peacefully find an amicable solution without the situation getting too heated. Remember: "There are no winners in a verbal or physical altercation."

In the past, I had an individual who came into our front office at work and was being extremely belligerent. When I approached the individual, I soon recognized that he was a drug user who was being verbally abusive to me and other co-workers. When I confronted him, he first clenched his fists and his body began to tremble, and the yelling and swearing continued. To defuse the situation, I stepped back giving him space and watched his body language ease but the verbal berating continued. Not once did I try to engage in any physical confrontation with him, but I did continue to make eye contact, listening and responding respectfully to his comments, always addressing him as "Sir". Ten minutes after listening and experiencing this threatening behavior, I stepped around him and opened the front door of our building while continually listening and keeping eye contact. He followed me out the door, tried to spit in my face, and continued with his tirade for another 10 minutes, until he defused and decided to move on. The key here is he was strategically brought outside while posing very little threat to the staff or myself. Could I have used physical force to reprimand him? Sure I could have, but would it have been worth it? Absolutely not. I became the "Willow Tree," using skills my karate training gave me to make sure this situation was resolved without any physical or verbal confrontation.

In the real world there are people who thrive on conflict and love a good argument. It has been my experience that there are some people who absolutely love confrontations, and would like nothing better to ruin the wonderful day you are having. First and foremost, let's not let these individuals get to you, and secondly, I am going to share and equip you with some wonderful karate-do tools for you to use next time you experience a heated situation.

1. Stay in control of your emotions. When you are in control of your emotions you are in control of the situation. Whatever you do, don't fuel fire with fire and respond back in an aggressive manner. Have you ever responded back in an aggressive manner when conflict reared its ugly head? What was the outcome? Remember: "Be The

Willow Tree (flexible) and not the Oak Tree (not flexible). When you respond back in an aggressive manner, your opponent will most likely get angrier.

2. Make eye contact and limit your body action. This is a great technique to use in everyday life. When your opponent is getting fired up, make sure you give them the common courtesy of making eye contact. Don't be waving your arms or stomping your feet, merely try and read your opponent by providing direct eye contact. By making eye contact you are establishing boundaries and you are giving that individual your undivided attention during a very awkward moment. By making eye contact you can often size up your opponent, and perhaps you can get a sense of what is bothering him.

3. Create physical space or an imaginary boundary around your opponent. Personally, I don't like anyone getting closer than three feet to me – nose to nose. If someone is displaying combative verbiage at you and is getting too close for comfort then calmly take a step back or two and repeat if necessary. Getting too close to a person who is angry can and most often will fuel the fire. When I am teaching karate students how to defend themselves in a physical battle, I inform them of three critical zones, which are the protective zone, the danger zone and the attack zone. Think of it as three circles – the protective zone is the outer zone and it's virtually impossible for the

opponent to penetrate and thus, it creates a safe haven even in the heat of the battle. The attack zone is the second zone in which you move out of the safe zone to set up an attacking technique. The danger zone is the inner circle closest to your opponent, that can cause you some real pain if you get attacked. A good karate student will be aware of these three zones when fighting and will utilize them to their advantage. I personally don't like fighting in the attack zone because I don't like getting hit. In respect to an everyday verbal disagreement, try and stay out of the attack zone even if the perpetrator is being aggressive and trying to close in on your space. Calmly back away and give yourself some space in your respective safe zone.

4. Speak in a soft manner to your perpetrator and don't raise your voice. Use words like I understand, appreciate and respect your opinion. This will automatically put the person at ease by releasing their guard. They will acknowledge the fact that you value this individual's opinion, regardless of how ridiculous it may be.

5. Be quietly confident in your approach. When your intruder notices the confidence that you have, he or she will often back off. Confidence creates doubt in your opponent.

6. Listen and find out what is bothering this individual by asking questions. Remember, questions get you answers

and could be an important step in the formation of an amicable solution. You may flat out ask the person – "How can I help? How can I do things differently? What do you think the solution is here?" Remember, talking your way out of a conflict is much better than using physical or argumentive forces. You win when you can listen and talk your way out of a situation.

7. Lastly, to the best of your ability try to find a temporary solution that will defuse the situation in a calming manner, and move on.

I can guarantee that you will be in a situation in the near future that will get fueled. That's life, but the key is how will you respond. Will you strive to be soft like "The Willow Tree" or hard like "The Oak?" When you come head-to-head with a Willow you will have some sway and give. If you come head-to-head with an Oak, the collision will be harsh and do some severe damage. Hence "Be the Willow."

Karate has taught me to a step back and confidently listen, relax and respond in a professional manner, even in the heat of the moment. These techniques will take practise, but with a positive attitude and a new approach to conflict, your life will be much more complete.

## 9

# Dream Big

**"Some of us know how to realize those dreams and others continue to dream"**

We all have dreams and aspirations, but the fact is some of us know how to realize those dreams and others continue to dream. One life lesson I learned in karate was to "dream big" and don't let anything get in your way. Karate has taught me that anything is possible if you only expand your horizons. I personally feel dreams can act as starting points, and then individuals need to make a decision and determine if they want to execute those dreams.

When I was younger, I lacked self-confidence but was a good dreamer. My dreams were vivid, calculated, and in my own little world, they felt real. The reality is, they often never came to life because I was standing in my own way. I doubted myself and never thought it was possible for me to go to university and get a degree, successfully open up my own business, be happily married, financially secure or become a black belt in karate. I see too many people get in their own way, make excuses and never see their dreams come to life. In order for dreams to come true, you need to be willing to take action. Once you realize what your aspirations are, take action by writing them down and start drafting a plan on how you can make it happen. The possibilities are endless and can include financial, career, business, travel, personal health or friendships. Your plan should be as vivid and calculated as your dream. Your dream needs to transition into a "goal" or "objective." Excitingly, it's your responsibility to bring it life.

Your very own personal goal will start to come to life when you begin to execute your plan. Becoming a black belt was no easy feat. I just recently had a conversation with another karate colleague and he indicated how very rare it was to have a student (from start to finish) become a black belt in our respective clubs. I would estimate that less than one per cent of students who start a karate program finish it with a black belt rank. It is astonishing when you think most of these students had a "big dream" of becoming a black belt but somehow, somewhere down the line, their dream totally fell of the rails. Bringing your dreams and goals to life will be no easy feat and I will guarantee you that you will come up against adversity and you may even experience failure. Adversity and failure are good life experiences that will build character. Successful individuals all go through these emotional roadblocks on their way to success. When you come up against odds, regroup and derive a plan to overcome your shortfalls but never lose sight of your overall goal.

When you take your very own personal journey through life, you will go through many different life phases. You are never too old or too young to dream. It's important to understand that your needs and wants will change throughout life but it's also important to always give yourself the opportunity to "dream big."

My karate career has taught me to "dream big" and not to be afraid to go after your dreams, regardless of the outcome. Make sure you have clarity in your goal setting and take action to make your dreams become reality. Just like my long karate journey through white belt to my 4th degree black belt ranking, you will come up against adversity in your respective endeavour and you may even experience failure. Everyone in life experiences these emotions, but be fearless, relentless and take action to make your dreams become reality.

# The Art of Taking and Giving Constructive Criticism

**"The objective of critiquing is to help improve and develop the student in a positive way"**

We have all had someone come up to us and give us points or tips on how we can improve in a particular activity. Many individuals have a very difficult time taking constructive criticism. They often get their back up and, in some cases, even feel hurt. The meaning of these suggestions can be more fulfilling if you respect the person. If the tip was given in a positive way and you respect the individual, chances are you will take it with grace and use the suggestion to improve. If the tip was given by an egotistic "know it all," you will most likely feel uncomfortable and not take the suggestion very well. Prior to my karate training, I admit that I was a bit of a "know it all" and didn't take constructive criticism all that well. It made me feel uncomfortable, judged and hurt. Often, my ego would take a bit of a blow. In short, I knew it all. Why would someone dare to tell me differently?

When I started my karate training, I soon learned that I needed to check my ego at the door and shift my thinking. It was okay for me to open up and get critiqued from experienced karate instructors who were full of knowledge and willing to share it. It was truly the only way I was going to improve. There has never been a training session that I ever went to that I didn't learn something new. Karate students are fully open to constructive criticism and the student soon learns that the objective of critiquing is to help improve and develop the student in a positive way. If the student is not open to learning, they sure don't last long and end up dropping out of class. When you are open to criticism, you are open to improving yourself and self-developing. It's a life-long karate lesson that has helped me improve inside and outside of the dojo.

In fact, now I'm fully open to criticism and I actually seek knowledge from more experienced individuals. In my business life, I seek business executives with the experience and knowledge that will help guide me through my business adventures. I take time to ask them for feedback on how I'm performing and how I can improve. This knowledge is often free of charge and gives me the building blocks to improve as a person. Seniors or accomplished individuals in any disciplines including sport, music, entertainment, history and education can help you become better. Don't always wait for constructive criticism, ask for it. Good questions will get you good constructive answers.

There's also an art to delivering constructive criticism to individuals. Your approach needs to be respectful and the tips need to be presented in a positive and constructive manner. Never be oppositional or disrespectful to your apprentice. It can be very damaging if it's not presented properly. Whenever I give constructive criticism to my students, I first focus in on positives. What are they doing very well? After positive reinforcement, I then address them on how they can improve their techniques. An example of this was a recent class I had with young Johnny. I started the conversation by saying "Johnny, you are doing an amazing job with your front kick". Then I went for the critique, "Why don't you try and work on shifting your weight to your front stance and you will be able to create even more power and stability?" When you are dealing with your own children, friends and co-workers, try this same technique. Be supportive and affirmative on some of the great things they are doing and then convey the constructive criticism to them. It makes it much more digestible and people tend to let their guard down and will be much more open to your suggestions. Giving constructive criticism is extremely difficult to master, but always think before you deliver. Be clear and specific on what you are trying to convey and always have the mindset of having good intentions on helping the individual. Be prepared though, some people just don't take it very well.

Karate is about continual development and constructive criticism is something that happens on a regular basis inside and outside of the dojo. Its purpose is to help the student improve and develop in a positive way. You are never too old to learn and if you are open to learning, it will give you a huge edge in your personal developmental journey. Closed-minded individuals or those who always have their back up will never realize their full potential. Always seek constructive feedback and be forever thankful to the donor. More importantly, always remember to pay it forward by helping others.

# 11

# Mushin - Empty Mind

**"It's a state where the mind is not preoccupied with any thought or emotion and is free and adaptable"**

Have you ever had stress or anxiety in your life? Do you have the tools to deal with these pressures or do you let them fester and allow them to control your life? If you allow stress to govern your life it can be very damaging and have a real negative influence on your quality of life. Life has challenges and can throw a lot of curve balls at people. The key, is how do we deal with them? Some individuals can manage stress very well through practises such as yoga, meditation, exercise, and having proper rest and relaxation periods. Others let it build up and essentially allow it to eat at their quality of life. In some cases, it becomes so severe that it ends up slowly destroying them. In the worst cases, it can turn into serious mental health problems. So, let's take a moment to reflect and acknowledge that we all have stresses in our life. Once we admit that this nominally happens to us all, we can then take the next step and start to formulate a plan. We need to learn how to deal with this destructive force.

Of all the lessons I have shared with you throughout this book, my discovery and understanding of the art of "Mushin" was the single most impactful concept I have acquired throughout my karate-do journey. It's a powerful tool that you can pull out of your back pocket anytime to help support you every step of the way. This concept can be very deep, but I will try my best to equip you with the simplified version, so you can start utilizing these techniques immediately.

Mushin is a mental state into which an experienced martial artist enters while battling in combat. It's a state where the mind is not preoccupied with any thought or emotions and is free and adaptable. Breaking it down, "Mu" means nothingness and "Shin" means empty mind. While fighting, your mind becomes empty and acts fluidly while having a total sense of calmness, creativity, and awareness. To master this state of mind, it takes many years of karate training, as most students have doubt, fear and anxiety when they enter combat. A karate master will enter a match in a state of emptiness and will be able to react to every move his opponent makes by being in this state of calm and control. Mushin will result in dominance and will destroy opponents with ease. The senior samurai sword masters in Japan often mastered this technique.

It's very similar to riding a bike – once you have mastered basic biking skills, you ride without even thinking about the technical aspect of riding. Swimming is another good example. When you are a skilled swimmer, you don't think about it. "You just do it" with a sense of calmness, awareness and fluidity. Many professional athletes, artists and musicians are known to be in "The Zone" while they are peaking in their respective activity, using control and calmness – "Mushin." When Tiger Woods was at the peak of his golf career and winning numerous tournaments, he was registering at this peak level. I challenge you to pick an activity that you enjoy and are committed to and try to practise it in a Mushin state – with calmness, creativity, fluidity and in a total relaxed and empty-minded state. It will enable you to perform at the highest possible level but don't be fooled, it may take many months or years to master. In the end, it will be well worth it.

### Me Time Mediation

*"Your whole body will feel totally relaxed*
*and completely rejuvenated."*

The second component of "The Empty Mind State" is even more momentous in supporting and achieving the highest quality of life that will help you deal with all the stresses and anxieties that we experience in our life. It's a technique that I have used for many years and it becomes a tremendous opportunity for you to personally take 15-30 minutes out of your day to "Empty Your Mind." I look at negative stresses or pressures as poison. By taking action, you are giving yourself the outlet to release these negative energies in your mind, body and spirit and allowing yourself to rejuvenate and have a clean start. Be selfish and consider this valuable "Me Time Meditation".

Here's the steps to "Me Time Mediation":

1. *Find a quiet and cozy place to practise without interruptions.*

2. *Sit on a blanket or rug and make yourself comfortable.*

3. *You can cross your legs, or if it's too uncomfortable, just sit in a position that enables you to keep your back as straight and relaxed as possible. You can also try lying on your back if that is more comfortable.*

4. *Close your eyes and focus on your breaths.*

5. *Breathe in through your nose (your belly should be expanding like a balloon) hold the the breath for five seconds (once your belly has expanded) and release the breath through your mouth (your belly will contract or go inwards.) One sequence counts as a breath.*

6. *For each breath, relax and focus on the breath - feel the breath moving through different channels of your body, hold for five seconds and release. Remember, the objective is for us to be in a total relaxed state.*

7. *Count each breath and try and get up to 60 breaths without thinking about anything. Once your mind starts wandering and you start thinking about something, regroup and begin your count over again. Remember, you are trying to achieve "Mu" nothingness, and "Shin" empty*

*mind. If you are a novice, start small and try to achieve 10 straight breaths in your first sessions and then strive to build up to 60 breaths without interruptions. Your mind will naturally start to wonder so don't get frustrated, just start your sequence over again.*

8. *Keep your body as connected as possible. Index fingers and thumbs should be touching, and your toes or feet should also be touching.*

9. *Focus on your breath and living in the moment. Be aware of your surrounding and allow your body to rid itself of all the daily toxins, to allow you to release the stresses from your life.*

After you have practised this breathing exercise, your mind will eventually reach a stage of "empty mindness" and your whole body will feel incredibly relaxed and completely rejuvenated. Endorphins will be released, blood will start to flow freely, releasing toxins and your mind will be free of the poison we accumulate on a daily basis. Muscles will be relaxed, and you will feel like you have reached a total oasis, free of everything. If you feel stressed during your work day, try practicing "Mu" in your car or your desk. Call it a "mini-mediation moment." These basic techniques practised by high ranking karate teachers and Zen Buddhists will give you the edge that will enable you to deal with the stresses that life brings to you on a regular basis. Practicing "Me Time Meditation" and the "Empty Mind" concepts on a daily basis will forever change your life, allowing yourself to be fresh and ready to tackle any challenges that are thrown at you in life.

## 12

# Learn to Read Your Opponent

**"Attempt to see through the eyes to see what your opponent is thinking and feeling deep down inside"**

Once you reach a high level in karate-do, you start to learn the valuable skill of how to read your opponent. Karate experts use this valuable knowledge to their extreme advantage when sparring. For the first 30 to 40 seconds of a match, I like to get comfortable and feel my opponent out. What type of body language does this person exhibit? Are they nervous or confident? Do they make eye contact? Are they slow or fast? Do they fight with their hands up or down? Are they a kicker or a puncher? Right-handed or left-handed? After I get a feel for the opponent, I can then start to derive a fight plan and start to hone in on his/her weaknesses and stay away from their strengths. This initial information is essential for getting a good result – "Information becomes power."

Let me give you an example of a past match I have had with an advanced 5th degree black belt. My opponent was a mountain of a man, at six feet, four inches, and well over 230 pounds.

He had over 30 years of training experience in karate and won many tournaments throughout his martial arts career. He had a very impressive resume and I was extremely honored to have the opportunity to spar with him. Saying that, he was also very intimidating to me, as he was bigger, stronger and more experienced.

When the match began, I made sure I kept my distance, knowing that with one blow he could knock me to the mat. For the first 45 seconds I noticed that he was slower than expected, did not make direct eye contact with me and kept his hands low. From that point in the fight, I used my speed and counter ability to move in and score points. As soon as he came in on me with an attack, I moved to the side and countered with a flurry of blows and kicks while taking advantage of his low hands. At the midway point of the match you could tell he was frustrated, because he was slower than me and could not score any points. At the tail end of the fight, his eyes told me that he was tired, defeated and had lost his confidence to an opponent who was inferior to him in rank and size. Without the ability to "read my opponent," I would have most certainly lost the match because I would not have been able to identify and take advantage of his weaknesses, as he was a much superior fighter in terms of rank and size.

The highest-ranking black belt will study their adversary intently and will analyze their movements. They will even break it down and start timing the breathing of their opponent, or will observe how often they blink. The advanced sensei will attempt to see through their opponents' eyes, to determine what they are thinking and feeling deep down inside. In some cases, they break the opponent through intimidation before the match even starts. Once all this fact-finding is processed, they use it to formulate their attack plan. For example, I have observed senior karate experts time their opponent's breath (or wink) and go in full attack mode destroying their opponent in a matter of seconds by timing these vital body functions. By seeing through the eyes of their opponent, they can also try to determine how that person is feeling. Are they totally confident with their skills? Are they easily intimidated? Are they doubtful? Senior karate teachers are very good at judging people's characters and it's a skill that everyone can learn from.

Many of us don't have the karate training that a senior black belt will exhibit in reading opponents, but we all can learn and attempt to read people better. You can often do this by making eye contact with an individual and using your senses to determine if this person is genuine or not. Listen to your intuition and ask yourself what kind of vibe you are getting from the person. If you get a bad vibe, be aware and proceed with caution. If you get a good vibe, move forward slowly and cautiously. Trust is something that must be earned. Many of us have built powerful relationships with family and friends over the years. These are people we love and trust. We know their character. The reality is there are very few people in our respective lives that we can put in this category. We must proceed with caution and create boundaries to protect ourselves from damaging situations.

Just like the karate student learns to "read their opponent" during a match, take time to think about how you can use this tool in your daily life. Try to become a good judge of character and attempt to read people. Use your senses. Make good eye contact. What type of body language does the person exhibit? Are they nervous or fidgety? Are they respectful? Do they raise their voices? Do they talk about others in a bad way? Have you caught them in a lie? Do they spread rumors? Do they exhibit negative or positive energy? Are they genuine and true? By reading people you will be able to get good information to make better decisions in your life. I see too many people getting beaten down by getting involved in bad relationships and friendships. Life is about making good choices, and just like the senior karate student you can become a better judge of character by reading people and blocking negative influences from your life. Create boundaries and stay true to yourself and the people who truly care about you.

13

# Resiliency

**"The only option for me was to get up off the mats and take the high road"**

Life can throw many challenges at you without notice, including health issues, injuries, work stress, job loss, family problems and even a tragedy. We all have choices on how we deal with and process these sudden adversities, and these decisions even have the ability to shape your life's path. Resiliency is a life skill that allows you to be knocked down, coming back stronger than ever even when the odds are against you.

Karate has given me the tools to be strong and push through the most difficult situations. If you make a life-long commitment to karate, it can be a demanding path which will put up many road blocks that you need to overcome. I clearly remember the time I lost my first sparring match. I felt deflated, humiliated, embarrassed and my self-esteem even took a thumping. At that very moment, I had a choice to make. I could have either packed it in and just given up on karate altogether, or I could take the high road and chalk it up as a learning experience. I decided the only option for me was to get up off the mats and take the high road. A positive attitude would allow me to grow and develop further as a student.

One fabulous lesson that karate has taught me is that "nothing in life is ever perfect." One of our karate rules is to "seek perfection of character." The optimum word is "seek," because we as karate students will never attain perfection, but seeking it and continually improving to be the best we can be is crucial in life. On the training side, karate students are continually critiqued on basic forms and techniques, even at the high-ranking black belt levels. We strive to be the best we can be physically, mentally and spiritually, without ever trying to be perfect. It's impossible. When we hit a bump in the road we are trained to find solutions and jump over the respective obstacles. Life will always be full of obstacles.

As an executive, I personally know what it's like to be the island. You have people and problems coming at you in all directions. The key is to be resilient and look for quick solutions that will solve problems and allow you to move forward in a positive direction. I had the opportunity to ask a successful CEO what his secret to success was. His answer shocked me, as he replied, "You need to be able to take a beating." As a high-level executive, he needs to be on top of his game because he is responsible for the overall business and has constant stumbling blocks that need to be dealt with quickly and effectively. We all know that one person who has been diagnosed with a life-threatening disease, has been seriously injured in a car accident or is handicapped. At that point in their lives, many of these individuals become resilient and overcome impossible odds to live a full life. They are the true definition of what resilience is all about. They have made a positive decision to overcome all obstacles, even after being seriously knocked down.

There is a strong correlation between successful people and resiliency. Successful people are optimistic and learn to face adversity head on. They are not afraid to fail and often reach out for help when challenges arise. We will all be guaranteed to be knocked down at some point in our lives. We need to challenge ourselves and believe we can overcome any obstacle that comes in our way. Be fearless and strong, and always strive to do so with a positive attitude. Resiliency is one of the best karate lessons I have learned throughout my martial arts journey, and it's a trait that has allowed me to be at the top of my game. You too can include this life-changing trait in your repertoire and arm yourself with the tools which will allow you to conquer any challenge that life throws at you.

# 14

# Enjoy What You Do

**"If you don't enjoy your chosen activity, you won't stick with it and reap all the benefits of your physical regime"**

One important life lesson that I have learned from karate is enjoy what you do. It sounds like a simple concept, but if you don't enjoy what you do you will naturally lose interest and quit. Over the years I have had many people come up to me and ask me for advice about getting themselves in shape through physical training. In my opinion, the single biggest factor to success is to pick activities that you enjoy. Naturally this concept promotes longevity and gets results. Karate is very enjoyable to me. I had the pleasure of recently training with national kata (form) champion Andy Pruim, who has over 40 years of karate experience. His first lesson to his students was you need to enjoy what you do. During our training session, Sensei Pruim translated his enjoyment of karate and his forms to his students and you could feel and experience the energy he was creating in his class. It was a very powerful lesson.

When people want to get in shape, many choose an exercise program or sport that they don't enjoy partaking in, and it becomes a burden. It's the single most popular reason why individuals give up. Not everyone enjoys lifting weights, jogging, yoga, baseball or karate. Some people like team sports while others enjoy independent sports. Some might like a hard workout and others might want more of a casual workout. Some people are competitive while others are not. The point is if you don't enjoy your chosen activity, you won't stick with it and reap all the benefits of your physical regime. In the short term, you may be able to force yourself to push through workouts, but long-term you will lose the zest and fizzle out. The great news is we all have choices and there's something out there for everyone to keep themselves in top notch shape. In my case, I cross-train my karate with cycling, golf, hiking, downhill skiing and weight training, all activities that I fully enjoy.

You can also apply the "enjoy what you do" concept to your everyday life. I see many associates who are in fields that they don't have a passion for, and are just showing up for the paycheque. There's an old saying that states "If you find something you like to do for a career, you won't work another day of your life." This sounds like a very simple concept, but a very true one at that. There is no need to be stressed, miserable and unfulfilled. Having a career that you enjoy is not only for the lucky few, but if you challenge yourself to explore and be open to change, you might just find that dream job. It sure does make life more enjoyable if you have passion for what you do.

I had a friend named Ryan who was a competitive runner.

He earned a full NCAA scholarship and ended up winning many races over his university and running career. Sure, he had the lean physical genes of a runner, but most importantly he enjoyed running and would train day and night. His passion for the sport was second to none and this translated to his strong training regime that provided him with results. When he graduated from university, he opened up his own painting business and he shared the same enjoyment for painting that he had with his running. I'm sure not everyone enjoys painting or running, but in his case, he was able to turn that enjoyment into a successful business and life foundation. Fifteen years later, I still see Ryan out running in the pouring rain enjoying his passion for running and I know his painting business became tremendously successful. You too can harness that passion.

Karate has become a lifestyle for me which I immensely enjoy participating in. It's fun and exciting, and I can't wait to go back to the dojo (training gym) for another lesson, even after 30 years of training. Too many people take the easy way out and give up. Giving up is not the answer - never give up. The answer is if you "Enjoy what you do," you will automatically find passion that will allow you to persevere and get the most of your life.

# 15

# Preparation

**"There is absolutely no faking it –
you are either ready or not."**

Preparation is defined as "The activities or actions taken that prepare oneself to be ready." I had the opportunity to work with a former world ranking tennis player and I asked him the question: What was your secret to success? What put you over the top? Unequivocally, he stated "preparation." Nothing else matters if you are not prepared. Like the old saying goes, "You get what you put into it." All the extra video, studying, dieting, conditioning and training will all pay off before the big match. It's the difference maker, not only in tennis or karate, but ultimately, everything you choose to do with your life.

How many of us are truly prepared for everything we do? Do we honestly dedicate enough time to prepare ourselves to compete at the highest level in our respective discipline? Do we have a plan? Is it written? Does it include goal setting? And most importantly, do you follow through with your plan?

Some people are masters in preparation and in most cases these individuals are high performers. They come from all walks of life, including academics, working professionals, business, sales, sports and arts. They put in quality time to master their craft and they get the results that they desire. Have you ever heard of an honour roll student not preparing for a test? I'm sure there is the exception, but most good academic students prepare for their exams. It's what puts them on top. High-performing individuals put the training time in to prepare themselves for their next big event.

A karate student must always be prepared to fight the next battle or get themselves ready to be graded to their next belt level. There is absolutely no faking it - you are either prepared or not. I participated in many sparring matches where my opponent lacked the confidence to fight due to lack of preparation. They didn't put the practise time in to gain the confidence needed to execute while it counted. I have also trained with many highly skilled karate teachers who have continually trained in their art and are totally prepared to execute their moves at any time or any place. These individuals are extremely difficult to fight as they have all the answers for a good offence and defence. Every move becomes second nature to them because of all the repetitive training they have endured over the years. All the blood sweat and tears that they have put into their training gets them the results they deserve. They perform their art with grace and complete confidence.

I enjoy golf and often tune into the Golf Channel to get my fill on golf tips. I'm often very inspired by how these PGA professionals go about their craft on a daily basis. They put in time at the range and continually work on all aspects of their game, including driving, putting, iron play, chipping and sand play. They also constantly work on the mechanics of their swing, pre-shot routines, conditioning, mental training and course management. If they don't prepare for their next tournament, there are thousands of world-ranked players who are one or two strokes behind them, waiting to take their jobs.

My very own personal karate sensei (Don Owens – 9th dan) never puts time-lines on belt gradings. He only grades a student (black belts included) when he feels that they have put the preparatory time in to pass the test. He often ambushes students and will inform them that they will be going for their next belt level at the beginning of a class. At that very moment, you have either put the time in and are ready for the test, or you have not put the time in and are questioning your abilities. Truly there are no excuses for not being prepared. Sensei Don keeps all of his students on their toes and through great leadership he teaches us to always prepare. Sadly, many students go years without advancing because they don't focus on preparing for their grading.

Preparation creates confidence and allows one to put the best foot forward and be the best they can be. These individuals will have vision and put forth the best effort needed to get results. Their journey will not be easy, and they will come up against many road blocks that they must overcome. Elite karate students use preparation (just like other successful individuals do) to push through their life-long journey in self-development.

Are you ready for your next big game, promotion, challenge or test in your life? If you were called upon to test in your respective discipline today, would you pass with flying colours? Just like the tennis player, golfer or karate expert, I challenge you to take control of your life and use preparation as a tool to ultimately be the best you can be in any discipline you choose to do in life. With the right attitude, the possibilities are endless.

# 16

# Self-Discipline

### "Nothing Comes Easy"

One of the greatest benefits of training in any martial art is learning how to be self-disciplined. Self-discipline is defined as the ability to control and motivate oneself, while staying on track and doing what's right. It sounds like an easy concept, but the reality is many individuals struggle with this concept. They often get side-tracked and are not able to stay focused. This impedes their ability to reach their full potential. I see many people procrastinate, give up or never really finish what they started out to finish.

Karate has taught me to obey the rules and systems, stay focused and never ever give up. Words like hard work, commitment, willpower, determination, self-control, strong-minded, persistent and grit all come to mind. The journey through karate is tough and it takes hard work and determination to be able to push through to the next stage. Life itself is often difficult and in order to succeed you must go through some very difficult times. As the old saying goes, "nothing comes easy."

Many self-made success stories in business or sport have excellent self-discipline skills. I just recently met with a very successful retired entrepreneur. He built an empire from scratch. He came from poverty, lived in an orphanage, was an immigrant to a new country, tragically lost his father at a young age and had people continually try and knock him down. He persevered and built a multi-million dollar corporation that he sold for a generous sum. Instead of sitting on the money and being greedy, he created a foundation and he and his family continue to give back to society. Without self-discipline, he would never had been able to achieve his goals.

High performing athletes, students and entrepreneurs also practise self-discipline. They get up at a certain time every day, are early for their training session, are committed and give 100 per cent at each session. They set goals, eat and sleep properly and are consistently putting in time to improve their respective discipline. There is no room for laziness, procrastination or a lackluster effort. To get ahead and perform at the highest level, you must be self-disciplined. You can have all the talent in the world, but the person who puts the most effort in will most often end up on top.

World Kickboxing Champion Mostfa Sabeti (who I personally know) has made huge sacrifices in his life by immigrating to Canada twelve years ago and leaving his family for a better future. As quoted by Nick Greenizan from The Peace Arch News, Sept 6th, 2019, "When you are training to be a champion, it's hard. You have to sacrifice. You have to watch your diet, there's training, and you miss alot of opportunities with your family". "Immigration is no easy thing, because you leave everything - your parents, all your belongings - all that stuff back home." he said. "When I came back here to Canada, I only had a thousand dollars in my pocket". Sensei Mostafa is an exceptional example of self-discipline. Here's a new immigrant leaving everything behind, pushing through adversity, becoming a World Champion and building a successful business in a new country. It's truly an excellent example of what's possible if you are self -disciplined and put your mind to accomplishing something.

Life is about making good choices and doing what is right. A self-disciplined person will strive to live by good morals and values and always try and do the right thing. Karate is a life-long journey that becomes part of your lifestyle once you are fully committed. It takes hard work and determination to keep you focused and on track. Self-discipline can help anyone get what they want in life, if they learn this valuable skill — sky's the limit. We all tend to get off the tracks in life, but by having strong self-discipline skills we can lift ourselves up and get back on the tracks. It won't be easy, but if you put your mind to it and stay focused, you will achieve.

# 17

# Never Let Your Opponent Know Your Next Move

**"Keep the cards stacked in your favor at all times"**

In a karate match, it's imperative that you are tactical and that you never let your opponent know your next move. It would be completely nonsensical to let your opposition know all the moves you will be performing on them, as they would be able to counter and defeat you. The true karate expert keeps all their moves to themselves as they always strive to have the upper hand on their challenger. This edge is often the difference between winning and losing.

This lesson can be used in your everyday life by controlling information that you may or may not want to share. Many individuals struggle to keep their cards to themselves and often divulge information to the wrong people at the wrong time, setting themselves up for disaster. You may be giving unnecessary information to people that will enable them to use that information against you in the future. Or you may be giving private information to a perceived friend, and that information is misconstrued and unknowingly delivered to others. This information then morphs into a rumor which can be very difficult and stressful to manage. Remember, you are the most important person in your life and you need to be able to put up appropriate barriers to protect yourself against any disadvantageous situation. Ultimately you are in control of your very own personal communication strategy, and you need to decide who will or will not receive information.

One of my friends once shared some information to his boss that was private and confidential. Assuming that the boss would understand and keep it to himself was a mistake, because he later found out that this private information was shared with senior management. The information was misconstrued and was perceived to give my friend a weakened image, which ultimately prevented him from a future promotion. In today's social media age, one wrong move could mean a ruined image and instantly destroy your future before you know it. Always remember to keep the cards in your favor by thinking information through before you share personal knowledge with others.

Some people also become extremely reactionary in heated moments, and say things that they don't mean and will regret later. Avoid this by being stoic and don't show emotion. It's like the old saying "bite your tongue." Silence will help defuse most situations and will give yourself the upper hand. It is important not to be combative. Giving your opponent unnecessary information could lead to other negative issues. Silence is a beautiful thing and can be very valuable in heated moments.

Just like the skilled karate fighter, keep your opponent guessing on your next move. It keeps people on their toes and leaves a bit of mystic to your repertoire. Next time you have important information that is ready to fly off your tongue, take a half step back and think it through before you share it. It's healthy to communicate with your trusted loved ones, but you need to determine who receives your most valuable information. Trust is something that is earned, and it takes many years to develop trust. By deferring information and keeping your cards close to your chest, you will be protecting yourself and not allowing people to use it against you in the future.

# 18

# Never Ending Development

**"When we stop learning we stop growing"**

Many people in our society get into ruts or even dead ends with their lives, without any thought or notion of taking personal action to improve as a person. People get caught up in the hardships of everyday living and don't take time to personally develop. One of the most important points I learned from my karate training is "Life is about continually developing as a person."

When we are younger, we naturally absorb information and lessons at an extraordinary rate. When we get older we can lose this sense of learning if we don't train it properly. In karate, "continual development" is a fundamental building block of this martial art. Perfection in karate (or anything) is virtually impossible and the advanced karate student is continually looking for ways to improve their techniques. They are constantly being critiqued and are craving instruction from their teacher. This foundational principle takes time to learn and can be quite humbling at times, especially when you feel you have just mastered a technique or kata (pattern). The reality is we will never be perfect, but constructive criticism is precious and it will help us move forward and grow as a karate student. Instead of being a know-it-all, we should all be embracing this powerful technique to enhance our lives.

When was the last time you took time for yourself and took initiative to learn something new? Are you open to new learning? If the answer is "no," then this is an outstanding time to seize the moment and make a small change in your life that will give you life-long gratification. Challenge yourself and ask yourself tough questions. When's the last time you read a book? Learned a new skill or hobby? Have you asked your music teacher to critique one of your pieces lately? Have you taken any recent courses? When was the last time you learned a new life skill? Think about it, there are 365 days in a year and if you take time to learn just one thing a day, you will learn 365 new lessons a year. That valuable knowledge will become the foundation of self- development and give you that extra edge in a very competitive world. Closed-minded people who are not open to learning can create barriers for themselves and hinder their own development.

About five years ago, one of my black belt karate colleagues inspired me by telling me he was going to run triathlons. What was really crazy is he was in his early 50's, and was determined to learn everything he could about the sport. He derived a plan that included changing his lifestyle and created a training program that eventually allowed him to compete in some very reputable events. Just like karate, he was open to learning everything about the sport and gaining the knowledge needed to compete at a high level, despite not having any previous experience. I clearly remember the sacrifices he had made and how open he was to learn everything about the sport. The daily training regimes paid off for him as he was able to reach his goals and get into top-notch shape, even though he was in his 50's.

Personally, one of the most significant challenges in my life was when I moved my family across Canada from Ontario to British Columbia for a career opportunity. The biggest sacrifice I made was leaving my Wado-Ryu karate club and an instructor (Sensei Bazeley) whom I adored. For the first six months, after arriving in my new province, I searched and trained with many different karate clubs and was struggling to find one that was a fit for me. I also was disappointed that my style was not widely taught in the province and it was going to be difficult for me to continue to develop and learn. One fall day in 2007 changed everything for me. I was leaving a soccer pitch with my family and I heard what appeared to be karate taking place in a nearby gymnasium. I dashed for the gym and was introduced to sensei Don Owens who was a 9th degree black belt in Shodokan karate. He opened his door to me and welcomed me with open arms, even though my style was different. Stances and basics were slightly different and all the karate patterns (katas) I learned in the past were similar, but had different components to them. The point is I had to be open to learning the new style, even though I had been taught differently, in a different style, for nearly 20 years. I struggled with this transition but was totally committed to learning the new style. Now I have fully adapted to my new club. Without question, this was one of the most difficult things I have ever done because I had to be humbled and unlearn different techniques and be open to learning the style. Without an open mind this would never have happened for me.

A dedicated karate student is very much like an aspiring musician, scholar or athlete. They crave and use their sixth sense of "continual development" to progress and master the skills needed to be the best that they can be in their respective discipline. Life is all about learning, and when we stop learning we stop growing. I challenge everyone to take action and embrace their own personal sixth sense by challenging themselves to be open to learning something new every single day – it will change your life.

# 19

# You Get What You Put Into It

**"To be good at something you need to work at it"**

You, and you only, know if you put 110 per cent into your chosen activity. I see many karate students who only put 60 or 70 per cent efforts into their karate training. They don't practise and are not focused on improving their skills. It's no secret recipe, to be good at something you need to work at it, as you ultimately get what you put into it. On the other hand, I see prominent karate students diligently work at their karate. They are focused, engaged, practise and put 110 per cent into their training. Not surprisingly, they see improvements, get results, and become very competent at their karate.

In order to evaluate your own personal performance, you need to be totally truthful with yourself and determine how much energy and effort you are putting into your venture. Give yourself a rank from 0 to 110 per cent and determine how much effort you are putting into your pursuit. Successful people are gritty, they work hard, and no doubt, put maximum effort into whatever they are trying to accomplish. On the contrary, I see many individuals making lame excuses about their lack of performance. They often make excuses and give every reason in the book as to why they are not making enough money, not getting ahead, or are not performing. The bottom-line is they are putting in lacklustre efforts. We need to be fully responsible for our actions and change direction to maximize our very own personal effort meter.

An example of this is my son Drew, who is applying for university. He is a good math and science student possessing a 90 per cent average. We both attended an open house at a local university and afterwards had a good discussion on his future. I asked him how much effort are you putting into your school today? His reply was 80 per cent effort. My response was if he made the choice to put in a maximum effort of 100 per cent, the sky would be the limit, and he could do anything he wanted in university and as a career. It's a personal choice only he could make.

We all have choices to make. If you are not happy with your current situation, you have the power to change it. The buck stops with you. You have three choices. One, to continue to perform at a mediocre level which will leave you trapped and limited. Two, is to take action by putting the maximum effort in, and changing the situation dramatically. Three, is to change direction and do something totally different. You are in the driver's seat.

Take time to evaluate your efforts and do a deep gut check to determine your personal level of performance. Don't be too concerned if your mark is low. Look at it as a positive on how much room you have to grow and improve as a person. It's no secret, good karate students as well as high performers give it 110 per cent maximum effort. If you are honest with yourself, you can make the choice to take immediate action to improve your performance in any activity you choose. By putting maximum effort into your given activity, you will be taking control of your life and realizing the results that you deserve.

## 20

# Giving Back

**"He is passionate about karate and he uses his 60 years of experience to give back to all his students from beginners to advanced"**

I believe we were put on this earth to give back and make the world a better place. It's a simple concept but many individuals get caught up in their greedy self-centred world. It becomes all about them. Taking time to volunteer or giving back to society through charity work will make the world a better place and leave you feeling rejuvenated.

Most karate clubs set the expectation for higher ranking belts to teach and mentor lower ranking belts. Teaching the lower-ranking belts is part of the development of higher-ranking students. Many of these advanced students volunteer their precious time to give back and watch their respective students flourish. In my personal experience, giving back to fellow students is extremely rewarding. You get to see first-hand the development and growth of each and every student and have a positive influence on their lives and future.

Some karate clubs are for profit and the objective for many of them is to run a business that realizes profits. High fees mixed with expensive gradings are the norm. There is nothing wrong with this model, but understanding the business model beforehand truly give you a feel for the club. The North Langley Karate Club that I train out of is a non-for-profit club and my sensei, Don Owens, is a 9th degree black belt who exemplifies giving back. He is passionate about karate and uses his 60 years of karate experience to give back to all his students from beginners to advanced. Giving back is his passion. You see this in many other sports such as hockey, baseball, basketball and football, where the coach volunteers his/her time for the betterment of their athletes.

I recently hosted a "Community Leader Awards Ceremony" where our company recognized volunteers who have gone above and beyond the call of duty to help others. Their respective stories were all very inspiring and it was nice to see the good others did in our community to make our city a great place to live. One of the award winners, who was a native elder, went on stage and said something very uplifting. He stated "Some people in our world are takers and some are givers - we happen to be givers." He and his wife have helped thousands of very vulnerable people recover during very difficult times in their lives. Giving back to people and your community makes you feel great, and it's an excellent way to make a positive difference.

There are hundreds of thousands of ways you can give back

to society and you don't always need cash. Perhaps you want to volunteer with your charity of choice. Join a non-for-profit club. Coach your favourite sport or activity. Or perform your daily good deed of the day like saying something kind to someone. Karate has taught me the extreme importance of "giving back" and helping others. I challenge you to use your talents, make a difference, and enjoy the experience of "giving back" at least once a day. Your personal contribution will be very uplifting and will make our world a better place.

# 21

# Connect With Nature

**"Although it seemed weak (water), it could penetrate
the hardest substance in the world. That was it!
I wanted to be like water" ~ Bruce Lee**

Modern-day life can be full of hustle and bustle with deadlines, technology, money pressures, greed, traffic and everyday stresses. Most people are in a rush to get going and are consumed by technology. They often spend most of their waking hours on their respective phones connected to the Internet. The majority of the populace don't take the much-needed time to connect with oneself or nature.

Karate has taught me the importance of taking time out of my busy schedule to connect both with oneself and nature. Martial Arts can become very deep spiritually for the advanced student, and nature is often part of that connection. Taoism is the ancient Chinese philosophy that focuses on being one with nature. Bruce Lee, the famous actor and martial arts instructor, is credited for introducing martial arts to North American and teaching non-Asian students. He often lectured about the importance of water and how it flows naturally and conforms to different shapes and sizes. In Matthew Polly's biography of Bruce Lee, (page 76), he published a college essay written by Lee that summarized his experience with nature.

"After spending many hours in meditation and practise, I gave up and went sailing alone in a junk. On the sea, I thought of all my past training and got mad at myself and punched the water. Right then at that moment, a thought suddenly struck me: Wasn't this water the essence of kung-fu? I struck it just now, but it did not suffer hurt. Although it seemed weak, it could penetrate the hardest substance in the world. That was it! I wanted to be like water. I lay on the boat and felt that I had united with Tao: I had become one with nature. The whole world to me was unitary."

He was often quoted as saying, "Be water, my friend."

Taoism can be as light or deep as you want it to be, but for many martial artists it's a path to enlightenment. Nature has many components, including water, wind, sun, air, trees, soil, rocks, and wildlife. By embracing mother nature, one can connect and find a spiritual uplifting and a profound sense of peace. Just like Bruce Lee referenced water, it can be a life-changing experience being able to connect with water and have your mind and senses feel all the attributes of water. Many individuals get caught up in the everyday stresses of life and many of these stresses can cause us poisonous experiences in our life. Connecting with nature can ultimately give us that edge to release stress and feel one with nature.

I feel very fortunate to be able to live and train in beautiful British Columbia, Canada - one of the most majestic and naturally-beautiful places in the world. We are surrounded by mountains, magnificent lakes, ocean, forest, clean air and wildlife. This beauty allows me to connect with nature and bring me back to a peaceful state. For me it's taking time out of my busy schedule to live in the moment and spend time at the ocean, or going for a nature hike. I like to feel the wind on my face and the sun's rays on my body. I like to hear the birds sing and see the calmness of the water. I take time to meditate and inhale the clean air. I like to ski the highest mountains and feel the powder snow beneath my feet. It's the spiritual side of karate, one in which you aren't physically training. By taking a half step back, you can start to experience all the great things that nature has to offer you. Your appreciation of your life and the world will be enhanced, and you will feel an immense rejuvenation.

Not everyone is as lucky as I am to be able to experience the majestic big mountain or ocean experience as I can in such a beautiful natural wonder as B.C. You can however take time out of your busy schedule to let go of all your stresses and feel one with nature. Bruce Lee, who is arguably the most famous marital artist to ever live, used this connectivity to nature to fulfill his life. You too can take time to out of your busy life and use nature to revive your mind, body and spirit. Start by taking a weekly walk in nature and take in everything your walk has to offer. Just like the karate expert, you will be able to give yourself a clean slate to fight off the outside negative factors that might be building up in your life.

# 22

# Be Open To Learning

**"Take time to learn new things and be the open book"**

One of the great attributes of karate is the fact that it is a continual learning process, one which no one can ever truly master. Advanced karate teachers often seek out a higher ranking sensei (teacher) so they can continually develop and improve their techniques. The advanced karate student, even after many decades of training, will always be open to learning and being critiqued. Reaching the ultimate black belt echelon can be a very humbling experience, especially when you find out you really only know the basics of karate and are embarking on your journey through this masterful art. In theory, karate can never really be mastered but advanced students embrace it and are challenged by the continual learning process.

I see many individuals in our society who are not open to learning new things. They often know it all and become very stubborn, rigid and set in their ways. They create barriers and roadblocks for themselves and their development. This is very unfortunate, because the world is a big place and there are thousands of opportunities to find new things to learn or expand your knowledge on current activities. On a recent business trip, I had the opportunity to work with a very young talented advertising representative who was still on probation. She was very bright and had all the tools to be great at her new-found career, except for one big problem. When any of her managers tried to help her and give her advice, she continually put up the blinders and had a "know it all" attitude. She had done everything, knew everything and was truly impossible to manage. As talented as this young person was, there was no way she was going to develop because she "did not want to learn." It's impossible to teach someone if they are not open to learning. Needless to say, this particular individual did not make her probation and really self-destructed.

On the contrary, my daughter and I went zip lining in some amazing canyons on Vancouver Island. We were hosted by a couple of indigenous people, who gave us tremendous insight on their land and their way of life. We learned about their culture and how they utilized the land for food. It was truly inspiring and spiritual. After our amazing experience we started talking about how my son and I like to ocean fish, but had no luck as of yet that summer. One native senior asked where we fished, and he was able to direct us to an island, where he said the surrounding waters would be full of fish at this time of year. There are literally thousands of Islands where we fish, but we took him up on his advice and the next day we headed out to his secret fishing spot. Within minutes, we landed two very large fish. This learning experience was very spiritual and was one that I will never forget.

As an advanced karate student, I realize that there is always someone out there who has more expertise than myself in many disciplines, including karate. I purposely seek them out and ask them to share their wealth of knowledge with me. Learn to push your ego aside and be okay with constructive criticism. Never take things personally as these learning moments could give you the edge and be the key to opening new horizons for you. By being open to learning, you are allowing yourself to continually grow and develop as a human being.

The Japanese meaning of the "do" in karate-do is "the way." In order for all of us to truly maximize our very own special "way," we need to be open to learning. Be like the advanced karate student who is like a sponge and continually strives to be the best that they can be. By absorbing knowledge, you are ultimately building your very own personal encyclopedia that will give you the edge in life and enable you to grow as a person and explore all the great things the world has to offer. One can never stop learning in karate and in life. Who knows, you could catch that next big fish!

# 23

# Be Aware Of Your Surroundings

**"This awareness that you will experience will ultimately become your sixth sense"**

One valuable lesson that I learned through my karate training has been to always be aware of your surroundings. Awareness is defined as the ability to know, feel and be in the state of conscious. It sounds like a very simple concept, but one that is very difficult to accomplish. This is particularly true in modern-day society, when we have many technological or personal distractions. In advanced karate training, we are coached to realize and use awareness as a sense that will enable us to always be prepared for trouble or an attack.

By being aware of your surroundings it will allow your mind, body and spirit to be relaxed and live in the state of the moment. Throughout this book, we have discussed many times the importance of living and enjoying the moment. We have explored Mu – the process of emptying your mind and being aware of your surroundings. How do we tap into this awareness state? One simple way is to focus on your five senses, including your hearing, taste, sight, smell and touch. Next time you go for a walk, attempt to live in the moment and take time to visualize your surroundings, be consciously aware, listen for sounds, taste the air, and take time to smell the roses and feel the warm rays penetrating your skin. Focus on your breathing and bring your body and your mind to a relaxed state. This awareness that you will feel will ultimately become your sixth sense. It will be your best friend and bring you to a state of nirvana and offer you a safe place. If there is danger in your path, it will give you warning signals, so you can take immediate action to bring yourself to safety.

I was recently exiting a building with a female colleague after an office meeting. The parking lot was dark and wet and as she approached her car she was startled by a man hiding behind an adjacent car. I went up to the young man asking him what he was up to and why would he be hiding behind the car. After hearing his weak excuses, he left peacefully not causing any issues. Looking back at that situation, it could have been a lot worse for us. What he was really up to we will never know, but by taking action and being more aware of our surroundings we could have had some warning signs before we were startled. Next time, I would take steps and be more consciously aware of our surroundings, and perhaps park in a lighted area to avoid any surprises.

By being aware of your surroundings you will be able to avoid obstacles that get in your way and keep yourself and others safe. Being in a state of awareness when you are walking or in a public place will reap benefits. Your sixth sense will automatically kick in and warn you of danger or uncomfortable situations that you want to avoid, allowing you to retreat to a safer place. By being aware, you can often sense people who may be looking for trouble or might be a bad influence on you and it will warn you to stay away. Awareness will also permit you to take the next step to allow your mind, body and spirit to relax and rid yourself of any poison that may have entered your life.

Many individuals in today's society are extremely busy and are caught up in the hustle and bustle of their lives. They become trapped and don't have time for anything or anybody. Just like the karate student, being aware in everyday situations will prepare you to tackle any unexpected circumstances that may arise in your path. Taking time to live in the moment and utilize your senses will enable you to become aware of your surroundings and will act as the sixth sense that will keep you safe and sound. Take a deep breath, stop and smell the roses, listen to the birds sing and visually enjoy your beautiful surroundings. You will be glad you did.

# 24

# The Importance of Goal Setting

**"New students don't understand that karate is a process and results don't happen overnight"**

Over the course of my 30-year karate career, I have seen hundreds of people come and go. Many start karate classes expecting too much, too soon and often get discouraged and quit. New students don't understand that karate is a process and results don't happen overnight. Past history tells us that karate started with only three belts – white, brown and black. A student started at white belt and for years would train until their belt showed signs of brown soiling (dirty), then graduating to the respective brown belt ranking. During their continuous learning for development and years of training their belt would become even more soiled and turn black, at which point they would become a black belt. With the old karate ranking system students needed to set their goals and persevere for many years to become a versed karate expert. When karate was introduced to North America, many clubs introduced a colour belt ranking system which involves several different levels of colour that a student graduates before reaching their black belt ranking. This colour belt ranking system is very beneficial for students to focus their energies on. They achieve smaller and larger goals which are vital to success. It's a method that keeps students on track to their road to success and can benefit the average person in attaining and breaking down their goals.

A goal is simply something that you are personally trying to achieve.

There are two types of goals:

1. Microgoals – These are goals with a shorter time horizon which can be broken down into hours, weeks or months. Microgoals are imperative to be in your plan to achieve your macrogoals. A short-term goal in karate could be to learn a karate kick, pattern or all the basic moves to earn your next belt (yellow).

2. Macrogoals - These are goals that take a longer time period to achieve. A karate student might have a long-term goal of becoming a black-belt over the next eight years. To achieve this immense goal, a student would need to set microgoals, by taking all the steps necessary to pass all the rankings, belt by belt. Other examples of macrogoals might be to attain a university degree, save $100,000 for a new home, get promoted or run a marathon. The possibilities are endless!

Goal-setting techniques could be your very own personal road map to achieving success in your life. It will keep you on track and show you how to get from point A to point B. There are eight fundamental building blocks to successful goal setting that I would like to share with you.

1. **Measurable** - Goals must be quantifiable and written down. Have a working diary and write your micro and macro goals down. Have a time period in which each goal is to be achieved. They can't be too generic, be as specific as possible. For example, "Your goal might be to lose 10 pounds of fat over the next three months".

2. **Action Plan** - What is your action plan? How are you going to get from point A to point B? Brainstorm. Using the above example, "I will achieve this by adopting a new diet and exercising on a daily basis." Break down these points. What does your diet look like? What type of exercises will you do? Record your results.

3. **Review your goals** – Don't cheat, review your goals on a daily basis. Write them down. How are you doing? Are you on track? Do you need support? What actions do I need to take today to achieve my goals?

4. **Have a support cast** – Build a supporting network to help motivate you and keep you going. It could be family, friends, a dietitian or a coach. Share your wins and your losses with them.

5. **Reward Yourself** – Treat yourself with prizes when you accomplish a goal. Take yourself to the movie or indulge yourself in your favourite activity or meal. Make it fun.

6. **Be realistic** – Be true to yourself and have realistic goals. Don't try to bite off more than you can chew by having unrealistic expectations of yourself. I see many instances of people setting too many goals or setting the goal post too high, and never accomplishing any of them. It's better to have reasonable expectations and a reasonable amount of goals to strive for, than getting discouraged and giving up.

7. **Persevere** – Have an "I can" attitude and don't let anything get in your way. Your biggest fan should be yourself and if you have the right attitude you can accomplish anything.

8. **Setbacks** – Everybody has setbacks during the goal process. Take a half step back when this happens, and evaluate what went wrong and regroup. Perfection is something that is not attainable in karate or in my vocabulary, period. We need to learn how to overcome these challenges on our way to achieving your dreams.

Goal setting can be a game changer and can be practised by anyone in all walks of life. Just like the karate expert, you too can improve yourself strategically by using goal setting in your life. The definition of "do" in "karate-do" is "the way."

High-ranking karate experts use goal setting to accomplish their objectives along "the way" to a successful karate career. The journey they take is not an easy one as they are continually coming up against barriers, but goal setting helps point them in the right direction and keeps them on track. By using goal setting, you can set yourself up for success on your "way" or journey through life.

# 25

# The Art of Listening

**"I realized earlier on that if I wanted to progress in martial arts I needed to start  listening and focus on consciously living in the moment"**

Most people don't listen very well. They often tune out or drift off, and don't take the time to focus on what their counterpart is saying. Listening is one of the most important communication skills you will learn in your life. Without it, you will get lost and not be able to attain your full potential.

When I first began my training in karate, I was a very poor listener. I would often find myself having conversations with people without absorbing the information they were providing to me. It was at times extremely embarrassing, disrespectful, unproductive and really limited my ability to grow as a person. I often found myself ending a conversation realizing that I absorbed zero information with no opportunity to press the rewind button. You really only have one shot of being attentive in order to get the most information you can out of a discussion, so it's best to take full advantage of that one opportunity

When I first started karate, it was very intimidating. You are training with individuals who have years of experience and are performing moves well beyond the ability of a beginner. A good sensei is willing to pass their knowledge on, if they have students who are willing to learn. As a teacher, there is nothing more rewarding than having students who are attentive, focused, and passionate to learn. Each karate class offer students tremendous opportunities to grow, but to get the most out of the class the student needs to be 100 per cent engaged. If students tend to drift off, they will lose out on precious development time and will often get lost very quickly. Karate is way too complex not to be paying attention and I fully credit the discipline part of karate for helping me improve my listening skills.

I realized early on that if I wanted to progress in martial arts, I needed to start consciously listening and focus on living in the moment. When I started to drift off I would literally pinch myself and bring myself back to the moment. I have seen many individuals with attention issues come into a dojo and improve their listening skills over time. It was imperative for me to recognize that I had poor listening skills, which forced me to be diligent and consciously aware of how I was registering and retaining instruction from my karate instructors. This improved listening process provided me the foundation to become an improved person in all walks of my life.

I recently had a conversation with a senior executive of a very large organization. I conveyed to him some issues that were very important to me as an individual. It was very apparent that this executive was focused on other issues and not listening to a word I was saying. The conversation was totally one-sided, and I felt very discouraged and disappointed that he didn't acknowledge me and my concerns. We all have had these situations arise where others don't listen to us and I'm sure they make you feel somewhat deflated. We can't change other people, but we can take action and change the way we listen to others, and give your counterpart the respect and attention that they deserve.

I would like to share with you some compelling listening skills that I have adopted over my karate path.

1. Realize and accept that you may have a listening issue.

2. Force yourself to be consciously aware and living in the moment while you are conversing with others. Try and absorb as much information from the conversation as you possibly can. Remember information is power and it will help you make good decisions.

3. After each conversation evaluate yourself and give yourself constructive criticism to improve. How much information did you actually retain? Rate yourself out of 10. How did you honestly do? After each karate class, I force myself to review all the information I learned and put it in my memory bank.

4. Introduce a trigger to get you back in listening mode. Shake your head or give yourself a friendly pinch when you start drifting.

5. Understand the importance listening will have in your life.

6. To improve, practise on good friends and relatives.

7. Realize that your listening shortfall is holding you back and is disrespectful to others.

Listening and giving others respect by being attentive is a life skill that will help improve you in every facet of your life. Karate was the discipline that allowed me to develop my listening skills and has made me become the best person that I can be. You don't need to be a karate student to be a good listener but take time out of your busy schedule to give yourself a true evaluation of your listening skills. If they are not up to your standards, take immediate action to improve them and your future.

# 26

# Know your Strengths and Weaknesses

**"When entering the dojo, they will use this knowledge to improve themselves on their life long journey of continuous development"**

How well do you know yourself? Do you know your strengths and your weaknesses? Are you using your strengths to build yourself up? Are you open to critiquing yourself and coming up with an action plan to improve your shortcomings? The great news is, nobody is perfect. With the right attitude, you can identify and work on a plan to raise the bar and launch yourself to success.

Although hard to swallow at first, (it can be crushing to the famous ego) karate students learn to embrace criticism from their superiors to improve their respective techniques. Without this valuable insight, it's almost impossible to improve in karate. Accepting the fact that we need to listen and learn is the first step in conquering flaws. An experienced karate student will identify and be aware of what their strengths and weaknesses are. When entering the dojo, they will use this knowledge to improve themselves on their life long journey of continuous development. Karate is a martial art that can't be perfected, and every student will continually be critiqued by their teacher to support them in their development.

In most cases, karate students have a dominant hand and leg. In my case, I'm right hand dominate, and I feel more comfortable punching and kicking with my right side. Without question, my right-side techniques represent my strengths and my left-side techniques are my weaknesses. It's critical that the karate student strikes a balance, so the left side techniques can be as strong and fast as the right side. Over the years, I have made spectacular progress on working my left side to get my techniques to a point where the average person would not know the difference. Even though my right side is still stronger, I identified my weakness on my left and worked very hard to successfully strike a balance. I have also been quite strong with my hand striking and my kicking, but have had some weaknesses with my stances. Again, I have identified these weaknesses and have continually strived to improve my stances over the years while confidently knowing the strength of my hand techniques and kicks. By knowing and understanding strengths and weaknesses, the karate student is able to develop a plan that will help them improve and become more adept at their art. This lesson can be applied to many things in you do in everyday life. By knowing and understanding your strengths and weaknesses, you too can come up with a development plan to strike a balance and exceed your goals.

The problem I see is very few people want to admit that they have weaknesses, and this alone is holding them back. I have a friend who is a world-class ball striker in golf. He drives the ball far and straight and is a tremendous iron player who hits several greens in regulation. Obviously, his strength as a golfer is his tremendous ball-striking ability. He definitely knows his strengths and is not afraid to tell others about his tremendous talent. The problem is he is a very below-average putter, which is his weakness. Instead of identifying and working on his weak putting, he has ignored this shortcoming and it's holding him back from becoming a really good golfer. Everyone should truly be open to identifying their strengths and weaknesses in every activity that you perform so you can develop a plan to improve yourself.

I challenge you to take a step back and give yourself a good assessment of your strengths and weaknesses. Take a good look in the mirror and use it to evaluate yourself. What do I do well and where do I have deficiencies? Stay focused and be totally honest with yourself, write them down and formulate a plan to improve on your respective shortcomings. It's also important for you to evaluate and know your strengths. If you are struggling, ask your close friends or family for an assessment of your strengths and weaknesses. Prior to karate, I was a bit of a "know it all". Karate gave me an outlet and the confidence to be aware of my strengths and it also made me comfortable with evaluating myself and accepting my weaknesses. By building on your strengths and identifying your very own weaknesses, you will be creating a recipe for success that will give you immediate lift-off on your road to personal development. This is one of the most basic lessons karate students learn and it can forever change your life. Do it for yourself – you deserve it!

# 27

# Repetition

**"You become very adept and the moves become
second nature  without much thought"**

One of the most fundamental lessons I have learned through my karate journey is the importance of repetition. If you want to master something, create a plan that includes continuous repetition and you will be sure to see some drastic improvements.

In karate, we are taught to continually repeat our basic movements and techniques to improve our proficiencies. In practising our karate kata (pattern of continual karate moves - like a dance), we learn the importance of repeating the moves over and over again. Perfection is something that never truly happens but by repeating the moves you are continually advancing and grooving your method. If you repeatedly practise your self-defence, basic karate techniques and kata, the karate student becomes very adept and the moves become second nature without much thought. When applied in a real-life self-defence situation, the karate student will act with confidence and grace. The moves become second nature. In fact, the advanced karate teacher will continually practise and teach the most basic karate moves to the most advanced students. In every case, the advanced karate student benefits immensely by using repetition to improve their skill level.

You will also see this in other athletic disciplines such as golf, tennis and downhill skiing. Athletes will continually repeat their basic techniques on a regular basis to improve their skill. World-class musicians continually repeat their pieces over and over again to become proficient. Good academic students become great by doing homework and repeating their subject material until it's ingrained in their minds. In all cases, repetition is a sure way to groove a skill into your subconscious mind so it becomes second nature to you, allowing you to perform with confidence and ease. The mind is a very complex organ, but repetition forces your brain to learn the activity by naturally ingraining it in the mind.

Ask yourself, what do you want to be good at? Challenge yourself by drafting a plan that includes repetition – like the old saying goes "practise makes perfect." Take 15 minutes every day or every other day to continually practise your passion, and I can tell you won't be disappointed in the results. Karate has taught me that anything is possible by practising and repeating moves on a regular basis. It gives me the edge to be the best I can be on my journey to continual development. You too can reap the benefits of this karate lesson by incorporating this rudimentary philosophy in your training. It won't be easy, but have an open mind and stay focused on your ultimate goal.

# 28

# Clarity

**"Unclear information will result in wasted time and it can be very damaging to yourself and others"**

When teaching karate classes, it's imperative that you communicate clearly to your students. Without clarity, miscommunication can happen, and it can often lead to unsatisfactory instruction. When this occurs, students end up performing techniques incorrectly. Instead of learning in a productive environment, they get side tracked and progress is stalled. Clarity is essential in karate instruction because there are so many finite moves that are performed. One unclear instruction at the beginning of the learning process could be detrimental to a student's learning curve

For example, when someone is learning to punch, they need to learn several basic moves to produce maximum results. Instruction in hip rotation, contraction, targets, breathing, fist forming, arm rotation and proper stances all need to be part of the learning process for a proper punch to be executed. One unclear instructional lesson can lead to that student being completely stalled in progress and could even result in serious injury to the student. In karate, you build on your processes and when moves or forms become more advanced, you need to understand and know all your basics. Clarity in instruction is key to a student's progress and success.

You can use clarification in your everyday life experiences when you are communicating with others. If you are the communicator, make sure you are totally clear with your instruction and if you are the listener, make sure you fully understand what you are being told. If you are not clear, make sure you ask clarifying questions to ensure that you fully understand. Unclear information will result in wasted time and it can be very damaging to yourself or others. As a senior manager, I often give instructions and direction to my respective management team. The good ones always clarify with me if they are unclear of the directive. The weaker managers often go about the directive in the wrong way and waste a huge amount of time and energy trying to figure it out. It's like going down a one-way street the wrong way.

I learned a hard lesson in my personal life when I received really bad financial advice from a professional. I wasn't clear on exactly what he was trying to sell me, and it resulted in me losing several thousands of dollars in investments. Looking back, if I was on my game I would have asked some clarifying questions and would have done some more research to fully understand what I was purchasing. It was an expensive lesson to learn but a very valuable one, as it has taught me the importance of adding more clarity to my arsenal. It could have saved me several thousands of dollars.

As karate instructors, we are taught to be clear in our communication, so our students can progress and develop. Many conversations that I have with people in general are riddled with unclarity. Next time you are having a conversation with someone, make sure they fully understand you. If you are listening, make sure you fully understand them. If there is any uncertainty, ask questions to get more clarity. Clear communication channels which offer clarity are essential for individuals to perform at the highest level possible, without wasting valuable time or progress.

# 29

# Leadership

**"You can't lead without trust"**

It's imperative that we all understand what attributes constitutes a good leader. Not everyone is cut out to be a leader and that is perfectly okay. We experience leadership through various channels including politics, work, family, sport or any team environment. Leadership involves leading a group of people to push towards obtaining a common goal. The big question that arises from the root of leadership is, are leaders born with leadership qualities or are these qualities learned behaviors? Through my karate training, I strongly believe that leadership qualities can be learned. I have had the pleasure of working with two of the very best karate teachers in the world and through their training sessions they have taught me some extremely valuable leadership skills.

Running a karate club is no easy feat. You have several different levels, ages, physical make-ups and competencies in your classes. As a karate teacher, it's your responsibility to keep everyone engaged while teaching your classes. The common goal is for everyone to learn valuable karate techniques that will enhance self-development for all your students. Good instructors will show strong leadership skills and keep students engaged, getting the best out of them. Bad leaders will not show good leadership qualities and students will soon become discouraged and lose interest. It's important that we all can identify good leadership qualities and exhibit good leadership skills when we are called upon to take up a leadership role.

The following are six rock solid leadership skills that I have learned from karate

1. Trust - Good leaders are trusted. Trust is something that you earn, and when you obtain the trust of your followers, they will follow and embrace your leadership. With my karate superiors, there was tremendous trust gained by their students and because of trust, students welcomed their teachings. You can't lead without trust.

2. Vision - Good leaders have vision. They set goals and they push their students towards a goal. For example, the goal could be to earn a black belt or compete in a tournament. What's the plan to succeed? How does the instructor set the vision and break down the student goals, so they can ultimately achieve?

3. Good leaders have rock solid communication skills. They deliver their respective messages clearly, listen,

make eye contact, inspire and use positive reinforcement to their followers.

4. Empathy - Authority figures have the ability to sense what other people are feeling and thinking. Through this sense they are able to adapt their leadership style to get the most from people. No two karate students think the same way, so instructors need to learn what makes a person tick.

5. Lead by Example - It's important that karate instructors set good examples for their students to follow. Do they have a good work ethic? Are they training hard? Do they exhibit positive, respectful and nurturing behaviour outside of the dojo? If the instructor leads in a positive manner, chances are the students will follow in their footsteps.

6. Charisma – Students are often drawn to teachers who have a presence or appeal. Good leaders make the learning environment fun and are all unique.

All of the above leadership skills are totally transferable for you to harness in your life. You don't need to be a president of a major company to utilize these important skills. At some point in your life you will need to exhibit leadership qualities. Perhaps you are a parent, or playing a team sport? The leadership qualities that I have learned from my karate training can support you in your leadership endeavors. Remember, effective leaders are to be trusted, have a vision, communicate effectively, empathize, and have charisma. If you are a follower, I encourage you to take a step back and make sure you respect all the qualities that your leadership is exhibiting. If not, you have the power to change your situation and become part of a team that exemplifies effective leadership attributes that that you can respect and follow.

# 30

# Refrain from Violent Behaviour

**"Turn the other cheek and walk away"**

One of our karate dojo-kun rules (club rules) is to refrain from "violent behaviour." This is a simple concept that many people in our world today don't particularly practise. Violent behaviour is destructive, abusive, hurtful, barbaric and completely unacceptable behaviour under any circumstances. History tells us that violence is at the front of many wars, gangs, crime, family abuses, religions and societies. Violence solves absolutely nothing. Life is about making good choices and violence is a destructive behaviour that we need to stand up and fight against.

As I have mentioned earlier in this book, the first thing people want to know when they find out I am a karate teacher is "Have you ever used your karate?" My response is, "I use it every day" which can be quite shocking to some people. The reality is I use the mind, body and spirit connect of karate to help support me through my everyday journey. It's always there for me as a guide willing to help me through the toughest challenges that I face. In real life I have never used my fighting skills to go out and violently attack an individual, even when confronted. We are first taught as martial artists to turn the other cheek and walk away from such actions. If walking away is not an option, we are taught to use the very minimal force needed to defeat your opponent.

Walking away from a confrontation is not an easy thing to do. The immediate reaction is for us to fight back, but the reality is nobody ever wins. In fact, when you react in a conformational matter you can make things worse by adding fuel to the fire. It's best to try and immediately turn the other cheek and defuse the situation by walking away. You can be the highest-ranking black belt in the world but if your opponent has a gun, a bullet will always win.

Verbal arguments can also lead to violent behaviours. If you are in a situation where you feel an argument could transpire, don't trigger them by arguing. These situations can escalate and become very violent and get out of control in a very quick time period. As karate students, we are taught not to ever engage in heated arguments. We are trained to have a constructive conversation with your respective adversary and be open to criticism and different ways of doing things. Your way is not always the right way and perhaps the person has a good point or two. Try and see both sides of the equation. Nobody ever wins an argument so be mindful when they arise and be prepared to have a constructive conversation. If it's too fueled, then learn to walk away.

Karate students are also instructed not to be in the wrong place at the wrong time. If you are hanging around the wrong crowd or are engaging in alcohol and drug activity, violence normally follows close by. By being smart and staying clear of these situations, you will protect yourself and others from unwanted violent situations. One of my karate friends was jumped when he was a young, talented aspiring black belt. He and two other friends were attacked by a group of about a dozen trouble makers. My friend was able to hold off the attackers in self-defence before the police arrived, but this unfortunate situation became even more scary and violent when weapons were drawn. The point here is they were in a bad neighbourhood of town, leaving a sketchy club at the wee hours of the night. By being proactive and making good decisions, they would have never compromised their respective safety.

Some people find themselves in very dysfunctional situations like bad relationships, where substance abuse can create a toxic and violent situation. People often feel trapped and are often vulnerable. You personally need to take control and formulate a plan to get out of harm's way. There are many people and organizations who can offer you support, such as family, friends, social workers and the police. You owe it to yourself not to accept violence and open a new door for yourself to live a positive life full of happiness.

Witnessing a karate expert exhibiting their skills in a dojo can be quite impressive. It's also very troubling to think that a karate expert would use those skills against untrained attackers. The true karate expert is trained to walk away from violent situations or at the very least use minimal force to subdue the opponent. Violence has dominated modern-day society and can be seen on TV shows, movies, media and video games. It often has become socially acceptable to society. Nothing can be further from the truth – violence is destructive and it can kill the human spirit, and humanity. An appreciable lesson that I have learned from karate is always "refrain from violent behaviour." Don't engage in conflicting situations, learn to walk away. You owe it to yourself to walk away - It's the right thing to do!

# 31

# Take a Half Step Back

**"I was clearly making decisions too fast and rushed"**

I have used the saying "take a half step back" more than once in the chapters of this book. It's a saying I also use and try to live by in in my personal and business life. As a karate teacher, I learned early on that I didn't like to get hit when I was sparring. One way I avoided this was giving myself extra space by taking a half step back when I was facing off against my opponents. I considered this extra space to be a protective zone where I felt safe and protected. It allowed me time to analyze my opponent and come up with a fight plan (a response) before I prematurely jumped in and made a mess of the outcome. This technique allowed me to maneuver and think it through before I responded with a successful attack.

I incorporated this very technique in my business life, because I found as a senior manager I was dealing with quite a few heated situations. These often demanded that I make quick decisions. Earlier on in my career, I was making decisions very impulsively and sometimes I regretted the outcomes of my decisions. I was clearly making important decisions too fast and rushed. I started to realize that this was a major problem and decided to start using my karate training technique of "taking a half step back" before I responded to important or complicated issues. These were important decisions that could affect individuals and the business. By taking a half step back (even in heated moments), it enabled me to regroup, clarify and think through before responding. That extra time (it could be a couple of minutes, or 24 hours) often gives me clarity and allows me to make good solid decisions that often provide positive outcomes. By using this technique, I'm making better decisions than I would have by being impulsive and sometimes regretting my decisions in the heat of the moment. If you personally are in a very complicated situation, give yourself extra time to make a good calculated and honest decision. Don't rush it or jump to a fast conclusion.

I had a manager who was very upset at a recent company policy that was made and released. Instead of thoroughly reading through the document, this individual made assumptions and then started to aggressively call out the decision-makers on their stupid policy in the heat of the moment. By taking a half step back and reading both sides of the document, this person would have seen that there was a solution to the perceived problem. Taking a half step back in this situation would have allowed this manager the extra time and space needed to thoroughly read and understand the document. By not taking a half step back, this individual made the situation worse by calling out senior management on a sound policy.

Life is about making good decisions, and we all make decisions on a daily basis that could have some serious consequences on your future. Like the karate fighter, by taking a half step back and giving yourself precious space you will provide yourself with that extra little bit of time to make a calculated and solid decision. Never be impulsive, because you will put yourself in a vulnerable situation that might lead to future regrets.

# 32

# Learn From Your Elders

**"I take the opportunity to become the sponge and try to absorb as much information as I can"**

My karate training has taught me the importance of respecting and learning from your senior ranks. Someone who is older and wiser can be tremendously valuable to your overall development. In my current karate club, I am very privileged and honoured to be able to train with high-ranking teachers who have accumulated decades of experience and are willing to pass that knowledge on to me. This knowledge, generosity and experience pushes me to my limits and drives me to be a more improved student. In karate, it's tradition for students to step aside and allow the most experienced sensei to conduct the classes.

In life, there are many examples of where you can seek this knowledge. Perhaps it's with a senior co-worker, retired athlete, veteran, grandparent or teacher. I purposely seek out knowledge from senior leaders on subjects that I want to grow from. I take the opportunity to become the sponge and try to soak up as much information as I can. It's key to fast-tracking and becoming well learned.

It's very important when you seek this knowledge out that you ask the person permission for a conversation. By asking, you are showing respect and letting your confidant know that you are truly interested in learning from them. I would also suggest that you ask good quality questions, listen and always thank them for their time. In some cases, you might be fortunate enough to tap into their knowledge at a later date, or perhaps, they become a lifelong mentor. Whatever the case, be the sponge, be open to learning and respect your seniors.

Without my senior ranking karate teachers, I would not be anywhere near the martial artist I am today. Their collective experience (over 100 years of experience) and knowledge has provided me with a launch pad to be the best that I can be. Karate has also taught me that life is a long journey that should encompass continual learning. It has also allowed me to be more open to learning new things.

I challenge you to be on the lookout for senior leaders who you can study and learn from. It's all about growing and senior leaders can be a wealth of knowledge and provide you valuable information that can lead you on your "way" (life path) to an amazing life. When you stop learning you stop growing. We should all have the utmost respect for our elders and take the time to listen and learn from their life experiences. It will allow you to fast-track your learning and enable you to grow as a person.

# 33

# Mentorship — The Sixth Sense Of Continual Development

## "A mentor can guide you through choppy water"

I can honestly say that, without mentors, my karate journey would have been short-lived. Mentors gave me the guidance and direction I needed through good and bad times and they always pointed me in the right direction. They set the goal post and provided me with someone to look up to and push me to become the best I could be. These guides can be instrumental in everything we do in everyday life, and could provide you with the inside track to success.

A mentor is someone who we can look up to as a role model. We can learn and model our lives around them. Life is a journey and we all have bumps in the road. Mentors can often give us the support and guidance needed to keep us on track and help us to grow. They often have real life experiences and knowledge that we can immerse ourselves in, helping to lead us down the right path. In my case, I have picked about a half dozen mentors throughout my life. They all had expertise in different disciplines that I drew upon including karate, personal and business. In all cases, I had tremendous respect and admiration for these individuals and I yearned to learn from them. There are two ways I went about my personal mentorship journey. In the first case, I searched for my personal mentors and had regular communication and advisory sessions with them, so I could be guided. This was in a coaching environment where I asked a lot of questions and listened intensively to the answers. The second way was I secretively searched out mentors. In this case, I would observe and learn from individuals who I highly respected by discreetly observing their traits and adopting techniques that helped mould me into a more improved person. In my karate calling, I have had two high ranking senseis who have guided and taught me through my karate journey. Without constant mentorship, I would have become stuck and discouraged.

You can also learn a lot from people you don't respect and don't want to model your life around. Karate experts often become really good people readers and judges of character. If they see someone who is exhibiting bad behavior, they are taught to use good judgment and not to engage or be influenced by negative vibes. The true karate expert is taught to turn the other cheek and walk away when conflict arises. By taking a half step back and quietly observing people, you will come across individuals virtually everyday who showcase unacceptable behavior and traits. Don't ever get caught up in the negativity that these less desirable individuals exhibit. Instead, use this information as a good reminder to you that you personally don't ever want to exhibit that type of negative behavior. I had the pleasure of watching my son's soccer team in a semi-final game. The game was close, but they did end up losing the game by one goal. After the game a player from the opposing team directed a racial comment to one of the players before leaving the field. This comment was totally unacceptable, and this individual was going to be getting himself in a heap of disciplinary trouble for allowing this unacceptable tirade to happen. The point is there were many young men who observed this behavior and refused to engage with this individual. They knew it was wrong and you could tell that they took the high road and knew this was an isolated incident. They processed this information and knew this individual was less desirable and they did not want to ever participate in such a disrespectful manner.

In order to continually develop, I would highly suggest that you seek out mentors who can guide you through choppy waters. Mentorship in karate is a must, if you ever want to excel in the sport. You are a small drop in a big ocean and your own personal mentor can give you the guidance and direction that you need to live a fruitful life. They will always be there for you, never judge you and will be the rock that you need on your road to self-improvement.

# 34

# Devil Is In The Details

**"One wrong detail will throw off the entire fluidity and proficiency of the movement"**

Have you ever bought something that required you to read the instructions before using it? Perhaps you purchased a camera, computer, software, or some furniture that needs to be assembled. Or you may have signed off on a lease or a loan. Did you read the instructions, or did you take short cuts and skim through them? Many times, I have seen people (including myself) totally skip the process of reading instructions and just dive in without paying proper attention to the details. This missed step never truly allows us to thoroughly enjoy our product or maximize its performance. Often, we waste copious amounts of time trying to mysteriously figure it out by not choosing to take the extra 15 minutes to get the detail needed to complete the task.

Karate is a very complex art and its movements are all very multi-detailed with many moving parts. This can include details like proper stances (which in itself is very detailed), weight-shifting, movement, hip rotation, torqueing, blocking, and striking to name a few. One wrong detail will throw off the entire fluidity and proficiency of the movement. That's why it's so important for karate students to pay attention to the details of the movements. When performing a front kick, for example, it's one thing to kick but it's another to study the several different sequential movements that make up the components of such a lethal offensive move. Any missing parts will compromise the effectiveness of the kick.

I learned a hard lesson in university that I will never forget. I went to write a three-hour final exam and I was feeling really confident with my answers. I can remember the exam being very long and I was observing others getting out of their seats and leaving the exam early. I thought to myself that they should have studied harder for the exam and I felt sorry for them. When I finished (three hours later), I looked at the final question and it stated: "Don't answer any questions on the exam – failure to do so will result in a zero mark." It was the first exam I have ever failed, due to my failure to read the detail thoroughly on the exam before executing. It was a very hard lesson to learn but a very valuable one. From day one, our professor was preaching for us to read all of our work over twice and pay attention to the details before you do your work. Even with the warnings, I failed to follow through. I had a similar situation happen at one of my karate gradings, where my instructor asked me to break down each movement in a kata (pattern). I was able to perform the pattern with ease but when he asked me for the detail and explanation of the movements he threw me completely off kilter. In Japanese this is called "bunkai" meaning analyzing the movements. At a higher level, karate instructors are not just performing the movements but they learn to break them down and understand in detail what the movements mean. When you do this, and only when you do this, you start to get a true sense and understanding of the techniques.

It's one thing to not read instructions and struggle with the assembly of a purchased product, but in reality, there are several different ways you can save money and time by paying attention to the detail. Have you read your credit cards statements lately, and do you know what type of interest you are paying on your money? What about bank fees, investments or car loans? Do you look and ask questions when you are paying your bills? Are you maximizing on the functionality of everything you purchase? I see many people missing important information that is costing them money and time. Just like the hard lesson I learned from my university exam, take time to educate yourself on details. My karate training has taught me the importance of arming myself with details to maximize my personal performance. By taking time, you too can maximize your personal performance and save time and money by being proactive and reading all the details before you completely jump all in.

# 35

# Learn How To Pivot

**"The inability to react quickly will leave you in a very vulnerable predicament that can lead to defeat or serious injury."**

With all the technical advances in today's world, businesses and individuals need to learn how to adapt and change direction quickly. What might be a common practice today might not be the norm tomorrow. With the invention of the internet, many processes have been disrupted and if you are too late in the game, you could be left in the dust.

In karate, we talk about the importance of a good solid foundation and how every move is built on sound stances. In the heat of a sparring match, you may need to react quickly if your attacker is charging you or aggressively attacking you with offensive strikes. The inability to react quickly will leave you in a very vulnerable predicament and can lead to defeat and serious injury. When such an attack occurs, we learn to counter, and part of this process is learning how to pivot our bodies quickly or change stances to get away from the attacker. By successfully pivoting and getting out of the way, you are able to throw your opponent off by changing direction and attacking from a different angle. You are avoiding the danger of the attack and at the same time you are able to counter your opponent with an offensive flurry to defend yourself.

Most people will hopefully never need to pivot for a fight, but this concept can be a very valuable lesson in our ever-changing world. Things move very quickly in our current society – the faster the better. Quicker cars, faster internet speed, lighting quick computers and smarter phones are just a few examples of these changes. If we are caught flat-footed and don't learn to pivot quickly, we could be quite vulnerable and get trapped. One of my former colleagues is a prime example of not being able to pivot. We had some technological advances coming in our business that required us to get some new training and change the way we do things. These important technical changes would enable us to stay competitive in our changing industry. Unfortunately, this individual did not accept the mandate and was resisting the changes which made it necessary for him to move on to another career. If he would have pivoted and accepted the changes, he would have been able to adjust and could have happily continued on with his career.

You see many examples of businesses growing quickly and all of a sudden they are on a down trend because they don't adjust (pivot) to their changing industry. Blackberry, Nortel, and Sears are all examples of companies not being able to adjust in a changing world.

We all will come up against adversity in our lives and we need to accept and embrace the many changes we experience in this modern era. It's impossible to change these massive shifts, so instead of putting barriers up it's important for us to learn to adjust. Just like the karate expert, learn how to pivot and change direction. If you wait too long, you might be compromising your future or setting yourself up for defeat. By pivoting and being open to doing things differently, you will enable yourself to adjust and continually grow and stay focused on your pathway to success.

36

# Balance

**"Too much of anything can lead to an unstable life"**

There are many meanings of balance in karate that can offer the student tremendous benefits in life. The first one is the importance of physical balance focusing on achieving equilibrium with the body. The karate student continually works on mastering their movements in a balanced fashion. The experienced martial artist will know where their centre balance point is and will utilize this point to maintain balance when performing techniques. Without balance the student will not be able to execute their techniques in a clean, fast and effective manner. Physical balance is often overlooked and without it people will struggle doing any physical activity or accomplishing everyday simple tasks. When individuals age or get out of shape they tend to lose their balance and will not be able to physically perform to their full potential. Tai Chi and Yoga are excellence activities that focus on core balance.

The second meaning of balance is the balance that karate experts continually strive to achieve with the goal of ultimately becoming well-adjusted in their respective lives. The Chinese Yin & Yang symbol is one that is accepted throughout the world as a sign representing all the martial arts. They are opposite forces, but when they work in unison they create harmony. They can have many meanings, but Yin is often referred to as soft and Yang is hard. Other examples are male vs. female, water vs. sun and light vs. dark. They are totally opposite forces that can be complementary to each other in reaching total balance. In most karate techniques, it's imperative that the whole movement is working in unison. For example, a basic punching technique has many different components to it, including the pushing and pulling of the arms. When the right arm is moving forward as the striking hand, the left hand is contracting, moving in the opposite direction supporting the move with speed and power. This same move should be carried out in a very relaxed state creating power only at the end of the movement. Both are great examples of opposite forces working in harmony (forward – backward, relaxed – power). In the science world, ecosystems need to have optimum balance, so the habitat will flourish. If that ecosystem has any abnormalities like an invasive plant or animal that is introduced into the environment, it becomes out of balance, resulting in a dysfunctional ecosystem that could potentially be destroyed. It's vital that all the moves a karate expert performs complement each other and work together to optimize their technique, just like a good ecosystem. It's also important that the same karate student strives to create balance in everything they do in life and continually works to strike that balance.

Many people in today's world are living busy lives and are often stressed. They don't take time for themselves and evaluate how the world is affecting them personally. Just like an ecosystem, the human body can be a well-oiled machine with everything working in unison, or there can be weaknesses in the chain that causes us not to function at the optimum level. At the very basic level it's imperative that the mind, body and spirit work together. Do you personally have balance in your life? Are you overworked or stressed? How can you better fulfill your life by improving your balance?

I enjoy people watching and I see many individuals who self-destruct and never create balance in their lives. Many people just don't take care of themselves. They are often overworked, over-stressed and out of shape. They don't spend enough time with their families and friends enjoying the simple things in life like long walks in the park. Before they know it, their lives can quickly spin out of control and lead to severe mental health issues like anxiety or depression. Even worse, these situations can lead to substance abuse, leading you the wrong way on a one-way street. Lack of balance creates a poisonous environment for yourself that can continue to compound. Always remember that the most important person in your life is you and it's your responsibility to get the most out of your life. It's imperative that you strive to reach balance in your life, so you can maximize your quality of life.

Many experienced martial artists strive to be grounded to the root and are very well adjusted in their lives. They create balance in their karate and their everyday lives. Too much of anything can lead to an unstable life. Take a timeout and evaluate your current life. Are you giving yourself the true balance that you deserve in your life? If you are not, take time to derive a plan. You owe it your yourself to create a life that is full of joy, and by creating equilibrium in your life, you will be allowing yourself to enjoy the things that mean the most to you.

# 37

# Build A Strong Foundation

**"Strong stances are one of the most fundamental building blocks of good strong karate"**

Throughout my years of karate training, the one fundamental rule in establishing good form was to build a strong foundation with your techniques. Karate has many different stances that are used to execute different moves or techniques. Strong stances are one of the fundamental building blocks of good strong karate. When you build a house that you want to last, your foundation must be engineered and constructed of good construction products. It's imperative that your foundation is strong and can withstand all the elements of weather, including rain, wind, snow, heat and temperature changes. If you take shortcuts and build your house foundation out of mud and sticks it will be weak and it will compromise the structure and lifespan of your building. Similarly, a solid karate stance will enable the practitioner to perform at the highest level possible. Without good form, karate techniques will be poor, easy to counter, and not at all effective.

So, what does a good foundation mean to the non-karate student? What can we learn from this? There are two meanings of building a strong foundation that I would like to discuss. First there is the physical aspect of building a good foundation. All individuals perform daily tasks like lifting, bending, twisting, and walking at work and at play. Often when I see individuals perform these tasks they don't utilize their lower body, especially the legs. Your legs are your biggest muscle group and often the most underutilized. Next time you are lifting something or twisting try bending your legs and feel the power that you can generate. This extra power will be there to support your movement and enable you to perform at a higher level, keeping you safe and healthy. When you are walking, try utilizing your legs more and have a slight bend in your walk. You will find you can be more explosive and stronger by using your legs.

I often find the amateur athlete not maximizing their true potential in sport by not using their respective lower body. Their technique is often dominated by their upper body. If you are a golfer, tennis player or baseball player be aware of your stances and how they feel. You will be certain to generate more power and perform better by having better stances. Good karate students not only learn to have a good foundation, but they build upon these stances and also learn how to generate speed and power through the rotation of their hips. Without a good stance, hip rotation is almost impossible. Elite athletes in almost every sport have good solid athletic stances and are able to generate explosive power. In baseball, golf and racquet sports, athletes are able to utilize fluid hip rotation in their respective swings, generating even more swing speed. The key is to never ever ignore your lower body as it's the fundamental building block of your foundation. Make sure you take care of your legs and include your legs in your exercise regime. If you take care of them they will take care of you, and offer you the extra boost you will need to improve your personal foundation for sport, play, retirement and everyday activities.

The other aspect I would like to discuss is the personal component of building a strong foundation in your very own life. Karate has taught me to look beyond my horizon and it gave me the gift to use karate as a foundation in my life. Everyone can use this same strategy, whether it be for family, financial, business, career, education, personal development or generally improving as a person. What measures are you putting in place to build your very own house foundation for your personal growth? Is your foundation strong or is it weak? Can you weather through the best of times and worst of times or will you falter during a crisis? Do you have an action play? Personally, I use the karate lessons I have learned through my extensive training to help me weather the storms and lead me through a typical business day.

High-performing individuals are tough and most of them have built firm personal foundations to help them excel in their respective field. Look at it as your very own personal supporting cast. Successful business people have excellent supporting casts that they can lean on. These may include a loving spouse, family, friends and co-workers, all providing them the support they need to continue fighting through good and bad times. Successful business people often have life experiences (good and bad) that they draw upon. They may use sport, art, theatre, church or education in their foundational arsenal. The point is everyone can build a stronger foundation in their lives and you can use this powerful tool to get you through the very best and very worst times of your life. Like a good karate stance, developing a strong foundation for yourself will empower you to become the best that you can be!

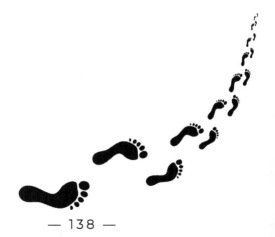

# 38

# Keep Moving

**"The secret is to keep moving...
we need to keep moving"**

I have been very privileged and honoured to have been able to train with many individuals who are in their senior years. Admirable, considering many people perform very little exercise or don't implement any physical activity in their daily routines. The result is their bodies naturally age and slowly deteriorate. This decline might include balance issues, muscle weakness, cardio decline, joints, soreness and weight issues. The reality is we are all aging and are fighting the aging process. I consider our respective bodies to be all unique machines, and if we take the time to take care of our engines, we can live a higher quality life for a longer period of time. It's kind of like taking care of your car. If you keep your car clean and tidy, change the oil, do all the regular maintenance, your car will last longer and perform well for you. If you don't, your car will not perform to its optimum level and it will start falling apart and won't last as long.

I have become good friends with several karate seniors who are very inspiring and have taught me the importance of staying engaged with physical fitness. One has just recently came back to karate as a brown belt and in three years, at the age of 74, he deservingly earned his black belt. After every training session, he looks at me at and recites his life goal to me "The secret is to keep moving . . . we need to keep moving." Not only is he in fabulous shape, but he has a great attitude and cross trains with swimming, hiking and yoga. My other friends are senior black belt instructors who lead by example and continually set the bar for me and other karate students. Sure, they could sit at home and do nothing but they choose to stay engaged, contribute to society in a positive way while keeping themselves in top notch shape.

By continually training you are able to build muscle mass, improve balance, increase your cardio, improve circulation and give yourself the ability to feel better and live a quality life. It promotes longevity and makes you feel invigorated and happy by releasing endorphins. Now I understand not everyone is going to want to sign up for karate classes when they turn 65. However, there are several great physical activities that one can undertake and reap the benefits of, including swimming, walking, yoga, stretching classes, golf, tennis and hiking, to name a few. I'm a big believer that individuals need to do a mix of muscle building, cardio work and stretching to reap the full benefits of exercise.

I would like to personally offer you four "Keep Moving" tips:

1. Find physical activities that you really enjoy doing. If you enjoy what you do it will keep you engaged and motivated.

2. Get to know your body and your limitations. By knowing your body, you limit your chances of injuring yourself. Remember, you might not be 25 anymore but perform your activity at your pace under no pressure. Don't overdo it.

3. Get checked out by a doctor to make sure you are capable of performing exercise.

4. You will be at times not feel like working out. Barring any illness, get off the couch and make it happen. I will guarantee that you will feel better afterwards.

We all know an individual who keeps their body in phenomenal shape. They work hard, are fully committed and never make excuses. Not only are they physically benefiting by performing exercise, but they are also benefiting by feeling better mentally and emotionally. My karate training has taught me the importance of the "Keep Moving" philosophy. Whether you are five or 95, you can still train in karate. Our bodies are like machines and if we don't use them, they tend to seize up and slowly wear down. When you keep your machine moving, it provides you the opportunity to perform at the highest level and gives you the quality of life that you deserve.

# 39

# Relaxation

**"Without relaxation your movements
be slow and ineffective."**

When most people think of karate, they envision students performing powerful and strong striking and kicking moves that can do some serious damage to their respective opponents. Little do they know that being in a totally relaxed state is one of the key fundamental building blocks of becoming a skilled karate student. Without being relaxed, it makes it virtually impossible to perform techniques with speed, power and elegance.

Of all the skills that students learn in karate, relaxation is often the most difficult to master. It takes many years to learn, as the student constantly needs to have top of mind awareness when training. Most beginner karate students will enter the dojo and use power to perform their new learned forms. Men notoriously use strength in training and try to uphold the macho ultra-ego. To them everything is about power, and they come across as being very tense and rigid in their movements. The reality is most high-ranking karate teachers are extremely relaxed and perform their respective techniques with fluidity and grace. Without relaxation, your movements will be slow and ineffective. With relaxation, your movements become lightning fast and fluid. Power only comes in to play at the very last moment of impact – "speed will always beat power."

Relaxation is a key ingredient, giving you the upper hand and allowing you to perform at your very highest level. Being in a relaxed state can be practised in almost any activity that you perform including sports, work activities, driving, social setting, presentations or performing, to name a few. It can give you the upper hand in almost every activity that you perform, just like karate. I recently attended a conference and an executive went on stage to do a presentation. He appeared to be extremely stiff and nervous and not at all confident in his ability to go up and speak. I was really embarrassed for him because he stumbled through his presentation and, minute by minute, he was getting even more uptight while his presentation continued to falter. Contrarily, the host of the conference went on stage afterwards and was telling jokes and had the attention of the entire audience. The difference was the host was in a very relaxed state and confident in his abilities.

Next time you get an opportunity, watch the swing of a professional golfer at a PGA tour event and notice how graceful and relaxed they are when they are playing. When golfers get too uptight or try to overpower the ball, they totally destroy their swing speed and struggle with hitting the ball clean and flush, resulting in bad results. When they are relaxed their swing speed increases, allowing them to hit the ball farther and cleaner. Elite athletes who reach the top tier of their respective sport are often zoned in and are in total relaxed states, allowing them to perform at their optimal level. Next time you have an important meeting or activity try and enter that meeting or event in a relaxed state. Rid yourself of all tightness, anxiety, nervousness and focus on being relaxed.

How do karate student accomplish this relaxed state? How can the average person reap the benefits of relaxation?

1. Top of Mind Awareness - You need to be aware of your state of relaxation at all times. Too many karate students don't even get to this point because they don't know how to relax. It's important that you feel nimble and in a total relaxed state. Next time you are participating in your sport of choice be cognitive of a relaxed state. Take this further and remind yourself throughout your day to be relaxed in all your daily activities. Whether you are at a meeting, taking a test, working, playing or digitally engrossed take a minute to remind yourself to relax. You will need to continually remind yourself, but it will be life-changing and improve performance.

2. Focus on your breathing – It's imperative that you use basic breathing exercises to accomplish a state of relaxation. When you are fighting (kumite) and someone is throwing super-fast kicks at you trying to knock you down, understandably, being relaxed might not be top-of-mind. Regard-

less, try and focus on your belly breathing. Inhale through your nose for four seconds (belly moves out) and hold for four seconds before exhaling and releasing through your mouth (belly moves in). Your body will become nimble, your tempo will be fluid, and you will move with finesse while exuding confidence. Try this technique next time you are standing in line, on a work break or before a meeting. It will make a world of difference and enable you to get into a total relaxed state for optimal performance.

3. Stretch - Your body is like an elastic band and if you don't use it will become stiff and very tight. Do a full body 15-minute stretch every second day. If you feel like you are getting tight, stand up and reward yourself with a mini two-minute micro stretch. You will feel rejuvenated afterwards.

4. Exercise – Regular exercise will enhance your ability to relax and release endorphins that will trigger a positive feeling to the brain. After you workout, your body and mind will become more relaxed and you will feel a physical high. Try doing physical activity that you enjoy, and you will be adept to do it on a regular basis.

5. Meditate - Meditation is an excellent way to release stress in your life. Find a relaxed quiet place where you can feel comfortable. Sit with your legs crossed and back straight (or any comfortable position, including laying on your back) and focus on your breath. Breathe in (belly ex-

pands) and hold for five seconds and then release your breath (belly contracts). Feel your breath and solely focus on your breath while emptying the mind of all the garbage. Try getting as high as a 50 count, and when you catch yourself thinking about something start your count over again. Feel your total body relax, empty your mind and experience the endorphin charge you will get from this experience. At the beginning, you may only be able to get to a 10 count, but practise mediation once per day for 10-15 minutes and experience euphoria.

6. Hydrotherapy - Treat yourself to a hot bath, shower, sauna or hot tub. Call it "me time" and allow yourself to release stress in your life and unwind.

For one to become an adept karate expert, relaxation is absolutely mandatory. Through continual practice, relaxation will allow your movements to become sharp, clean and lightning fast. It's a process that will take years to master but it will allow the karate student to become the best they can be. It's a technique that can be totally transferable to your everyday activities and will allow you to grow as a person. Without relaxation you will be fighting yourself, as you become stiff, stressed and often unproductive.

Relaxation should be top of mind for you in all of your activities. By using the above methods just like the karate expert, you will be releasing unwanted tension, giving you the edge that you deserve in the very stressful world that we live in.

# 40

# Stay Loose

### "If you don't use it you lose it"

Stretching has been a key pillar in my karate training throughout the years. Without it, I would not have been able to continually progress with the challenging movements that my sport demands. Stretching is often overlooked by strength conditioning or cardiovascular training, but it's just as important. Not everyone is going to need to stretch at the level of a martial artist or gymnast, but everyone can take advantage and enjoy the numerous benefits stretching has to offer.

I look at the body as an elastic and when you take time to stretch, your body lengthens the muscles and tendons that attach to the bone. The results are invigorating as the body becomes loose, relaxed and mobile. If you don't stretch, the elastic becomes tight and you start to lose mobility. As the old saying goes "If you don't use it you lose it." There are several benefits to stretching, including: increased blood flow and circulation, improved balance, injury prevention, tension and stress relief, promotion of relaxation, and bringing you a full range of motion that helps you with bending, twisting, and lifting motions.

I don't believe you need to go overboard with your stretching. If you could find 10-15 minutes every other day, you will begin to reap the benefits. Here are some of my stretching tips directly from my karate classes.

1. Focus on your breathing when you are performing your stretch and don't hold your breath. To optimize your stretch, take a full breath in (expand your belly) and when you lengthen the stretch slowly exhale. Proper breathing will lengthen your stretch and make it much more pleasant.

2. No bouncing. Make slow controlled moves. Bouncing promotes ripping and tearing. Never force the stretch.

3. Warm up your body before you perform your stretch. Try doing 5-10 minutes of running, jumping-jacks, or skipping. This will get the blood moving and your body warm before you begin your routine.

4. Create a full body stretching program that suits your needs and your lifestyle. Make sure it's a full body stretch that include everything from your toes to your nose. Don't forget your mouth, face, and eyes. Shoulders, legs, neck, and back are all vulnerable areas that become stressed and tight and do need to be included in your routine.

5. Create a mini-body stretching routine that you can per-

form at your office desk or on a quick break.

6. Warm down with 5-10 minutes of cardio.

7. There has been debate on whether it's better to perform your stretching before or after a physical activity. I personally think it's better to do a light stretch before and after a physical activity. Make it part of your routine.

8. Be patient. You may not be able to touch your toes overnight but that's totally okay. Take your time and you will see progress.

When I first started taking karate, I was super tight and often experienced back and neck pain. In fact, I could not bend down to touch my toes. Karate has taught me the importance of staying loose and stretching my muscles to get the most out of my body. It's like giving yourself a full body tune-up every time you take time to stretch. It's one of the most underrated and under-appreciated physical activities which helps support a long active lifestyle. Just like a karate expert, give yourself the gift of a good stretch and I promise you it will provide you with the proper maintenance routine that will support an active and improved lifestyle.

41

# Core Karate Training

In karate, strengthening your core is an essential part of the conditioning routine that enables you to participate and perform all the kicking, punching and twisting moves needed to be the best you can be at your art. It improves balance and creates stability, supporting the strong foundation needed for stances and fundamental basics. Compare it to a solid foundation that will support a well-built home through the best and very worst elements mother nature has to offer it. The house will withstand strong winds, rain, temperature changes and will keep you warm and safe. Without a strong foundation, your entire house is at risk of breaking or falling over. Whether you are an experienced karate instructor or an everyday average person, a strong core is an essential building block to a healthy lifestyle.

My definition of core is all the abdominal muscles supporting the midsection of your body, including the front, side and back section. The core acts as a stabilizer for your everyday activities, which include walking, twisting, bending and lifting. Without a strong core you can be prone to many different injuries, including back or muscle injuries. You will also naturally suffer from a lack of balance. In karate, the core is needed to perform strong karate techniques. Likewise, the core is essential for everyone to participate in everyday average activities. Just think how many times you unconsciously use your core to perform everyday tasks. It starts when you wake up in the morning and use your core muscles to roll out of bed. Walking down the stairs to eat breakfast requires a strong core. Turning your body and reaching for the milk on the table requires a strong core as well as bending over and picking up the spoon you just dropped on the floor. Getting in the bathtub, dressing, brushing your teeth, walking and putting on your shoes all require strong core muscles.

The important point to note is a strong core is very essential for you to perform your everyday activities safely. So now that we all are convinced that a strong core is important, what actions can we take to build it up? There are several different exercises that you can perform to accomplish this, but I will give you my favourite four that I regularly include in my exercise regime.

1. Push-ups – I have observed many individuals being sloppy and using bad techniques when performing push-ups. Technique is essential if you want to reap the benefits of this fine exercise. Keep the body straight (including your butt) and bend at the elbows lowering your body slowly to the ground (but not touching the ground). Slowly raise your body to the starting position. Focus on your breath-

ing. Inhale when you lower yourself and exhale when you are lifting. If you are not strong enough to do a proper push-up try doing them on your knees which will take the weight off the push-up. Proper form is most important. Try doing as many as you can for three sets and keep building slowly from there. Push-ups are one of my favourite exercises because you don't need equipment, can do them anywhere, and they literally work all your muscle groups including the core. Once you are in total control of your movement try moving your hand position to a wider or narrower position working still different muscles. More advanced individuals can try a slow count while performing a push-up. Try counting to 10 slowly on one of your push-ups. The count should be five on the way down and five on the way up. The movement should be controlled and slow. This movement will feel more challenging and will give you an advance exercise that you can use to further build strength.

2. Planks – Planks are absolutely fantastic for building your core. Just like a push-up, keep your body straight and slowly lower yourself so your weight is distributed on your forearms and your toes. Simply, you will create a bridge effect. Focus on your breathing and start your very own personal count. For my advanced students, we will count slowly to 100 and then count backwards until we reach zero. Try keeping your mind in a different place like your favourite beach. Never focus on the pain or your mind will

play games with you and you will end up collapsing sooner. If you are a beginner, try going on your knees which will take the pressure and weight off you. Start really slow by counting to 10 for three sets. The goal is to improve the count every time. This exercise will really make you work and you will feel every muscle in your core engaged.

3. Crunch – My variation of a crunch is different from your standard crunch and is essential in my core building routine. Lay flat on your back with your knees up. Rest your finger tips to the side of your head (Don't put them behind your head because the pressure can leave you with possible neck issues). While on your back inhale and raise your shoulders off the floor while exhaling. Touch both elbows to your knees, then hold for two seconds. Slowly release and your shoulders will touch the floor. The key is to never disengage or relax your abs. Repeat the movement and try and do as many as you can while never compromising your form. When you are raising or lowering your body find a visual spot on the wall in front of you and have that as your focal point during the entire set. This will keep you in the optimal position and give you great results. Try building up to three to five sets, with 10-20 reps per set - improving your count with each session. Advanced students can slow the count down or make a count for each movement up and down. For example, slowly count to 10 on the way up and slowly count to 10 on the way down, keeping fully engaged during the session.

4. Twist Crunch - The twist crunch is a variation of the above crunch. Lay on your back with your knees up. Rest your finger tips to the side of your head. Inhale while on your back and exhale, slowly raising your right shoulder and touching your right elbow to your left knee. Keep the core engaged and slowly bring down your shoulder to the floor while keeping abs fully engaged. Repeat the steps to the opposite way.

A strong core is essential for an advanced karate student to perform at a high level. With all the bending and twisting that is required in the sport, your core must be prepared to support you on every move you make. It also protects you from injury when you get hit or kicked in the mid-section. It also acts as an important catalyst to generate power. The average person will not use their respective core for practising karate, but by keeping your very own core strong you will be able to perform and get more out of your daily activities. If you take care of your core, it will take care of you as it will add to the quality of your life by allowing you to expand your horizon and try different activities for many years to come.

# 42

# You Are What You Eat

I don't pretend to be a nutritionist or a doctor, but I do believe we become what we eat. As a karate practitioner you make sacrifices and part of that is being disciplined and making sure we feed our bodies properly. You are only fooling yourself if you don't, and your performance will suffer if you don't give your body the nutritional balance it needs to perform. I look at eating and dieting as fueling your body. Without good fuel your vehicle will not run properly, and it will become sluggish. If your diet is packed with junk, then your body will not run properly, and it will also feel sluggish not allowing you to perform. You don't see too many high performing athletes who are several pounds overweight.

As a karate student it's my goal to eat a balance nutritional diet full of fruit and vegetables. There are several thousand programs or ways to eat in our world today, but your goal should be to find a diet that will work for you and your lifestyle. I'm not going to go into what you should eat because I believe that is beyond my scope of expertise. However, I can't emphasize on how important it is to find a diet that will give you the edge in life that you need. Remember to always treat yourself and give yourself that reward that you deserve for following your very own program. Pack a lunch and visit your local farm market to enjoy the latest and greatest rounds of fruits and vegetables of the season. Stay away from processed food, too much sugar and limit the amount of time you eat out. By making your own meals you are controlling what your intake is and thus, giving you the energy you need. My last advice is to stay hydrated with water throughout the day whether at work, play or doing physical activity. Staying hydrated will allow you to perform at your optimal level.

# 43

# Self-Reliant — "It's Up To You"

The great thing about life is you are in the driver seat and can make anything happen if you are focused and put your mind to it. Karate has demonstrated the importance to me of being out on the edge and totally exposed to the world. When I'm in the ring and fighting my opponent, there is nobody that can help me but myself, it's what I like about individual sports like golf, track and tennis. You become totally trusted in the skills you have acquired, and you learn to be self-reliant. You are guided by yourself and you have nobody to blame but yourself for winning or losing. You have either put the necessary work in to be successful or you have not.

Individuals that are too reliant on others will live their life in a bubble and will never be able to realize the full potential that they have. I see many marriages where one spouse dominates the other by making all the decisions and controlling the life of their respective spouse. The individual that is controlled is the one that will feel trapped and never be able to grow. They will never have the luxury of feeling empowered and getting the most out of their life by controlling their very own destiny. Controlling your "own way" will be extremely rewarding and give you the fulfilment you deserve to become the best that you can become. This incredible driving force needs to come within yourself. You need to become totally dependent on yourself when you enter the ring just like the karate fighter. In the end, you are the only person that can make yourself be successful.

I challenge you to be self-reliant just like the experienced karate teacher and make your dreams become reality. All of the lessons that I shared in the pages of this book requires you to become self-reliant. You will either take initiative and be in the driver seat or you will allow others to drive the car for you. It's your personal decision. By taking action you will be able to take control of your life and never ever need to rely on anyone to make it happen for you.

# 44

# Conclusion

I would like to personally thank you taking the time out of your busy schedule to join me on your personal journey through the "Mojo in The Karate Dojo" book. When I first decided to put these thoughts into a book format, my goal was to help each and every reader with fruitful and simple advice that you could use in your personal life, things I have learned through my karate training. I fully understand that many of these concepts that you read in this book are not foreign to you and you may be using some of them in your current voyage through life. If you have only learned one or two things from the readings and the others are good refreshers for you, I consider my writings to be a success.

Karate has not only given me the ability to learn how to defend myself and others, it has provided me with a pivotal foundation of life lessons that has changed my life forever. Whether it's a reminder to think with a positive mind, be the willow tree in the heat of the moment or take a half step back and evaluate the situation before responding, they are all good concepts that will help nurture you through your personal journey. I trust that you enjoyed these karate lessons and that you will take time to incorporate some "Mojo" in your life. It's your life to live and good sound advice will help you along "your way or path" of personal success. You will have some bumps and bruises along the way, but stay focused and use this book as a tool to always get you back on the tracks. I trust that my mojo from the Karate Dojo will inspire you to get the most out of life and be the best you can possibly be.

# Glossary

**Karate** – A Japanese system of unarmed combat using hands and feet to deliver kicks, strikes and blocks. Was founded in Okinawa in the 17th century and popularized in Japan in the early 1900's.

**Karate-do** – The word karate is a combination of two Chinese characters: Kara, meaning empty and te means hand: thus, the definition empty hand. The do translates to the "The way or path".

**Shotokan Karate** – Is one of the most popular styles of karate created by Gichin Funakoshi in the late 1800's.

**Wado-Ryu Karate** – One of the four major karate styles founded by Hironori Otsuka in 1939. It's a branch from Shotokan karate and Jujutsu.

**Dojo** – A special place and gym where karate students train.

**Sensei** – Teacher.

**Hanshi** – A very high-ranking karate teacher.

**Martial Arts** – Forms of self defense sports that include disciplines such as Judo, Karate, Kendo, Kung-Fu and Kick Boxing to name a few.

**Martial Artist** – Someone who trains in a martial arts discipline.

**Black Belt** – A belt worn by martial artist that is earned over many years of training. There are ten degrees (levels) of black belt in karate that go from first degree (beginner level) to the most advance level which is tenth.

**Kime** – Means power or in karate focus and energy.

**Kata** – A series of karate techniques that are learned. A kata is like a dance.

**Kumite** – Fighting or sparring.

**Doju Kun** – Karate club rules.

**Mushin** – A mental state into which a martial artist enters while training. A state where the mind is free of emotion.

**WJKA** – World Japan Karate Association.